Office 95
Made Simple

Made Simple *Computer Books*

● **easy to follow**   ● **jargon free**   ● **practical**   ● **task based**   ● **easy steps**

Thousands of people have already discovered that the **MADE SIMPLE** series gives them what they want *fast!* These are the books for you if you want to **learn quickly what's essential** and **how** to do things with a particular piece of software.

Many delighted readers have written, telephone and e-mailed us about the **Made Simple Series** of Computer books. Comments have included:

● "Clear, concise and well laid out."

● "Ideal for the first time user."

● "Clear, accurate, well presented, jargon free, well targeted."

● "Easy to follow to perform a task."

● "Ilustrations are excellent."

● "I haven't found any other books worth recommending until these."

This **best selling** series is in your **local bookshop now**, or in case of difficulty, contact:

Reed Book Services Ltd., Orders Dept, PO Box 5, Rushden, Northants, NN10 9YX.
Tel 01933 58521. Fax 01933 50284. Credit card sales 01933 414000.

Series titles:

Excel for Windows	Stephen Morris	0 7506 2070 6
Lotus 1-2-3 (DOS)	Ian Robertson	0 7506 2066 8
MS-DOS	Ian Sinclair	0 7506 2069 2
MS-Works for Windows	P. K. McBride	0 7506 2065 X
Windows 3.1	P. K. McBride	0 7506 2072 2
Word for Windows	Keith Brindley	0 7506 2071 4
WordPerfect (DOS)	Stephen Copestake	0 7506 2068 4
Access for Windows	Moira Stephen	0 7506 2309 8
The Internet	P.K.McBride	0 7506 2311 X
Quicken for Windows	Stephen Copestake	0 7506 2308 X
WordPerfect for Windows	Keith Brindley	0 7506 2310 1
Lotus 123 (5.0) for Windows	Stephen Morris	0 7506 2307 1
Multimedia	Simon Collin	0 7506 2314 4
Pageplus for Windows	Ian Sinclair	0 7506 2312 8
Powerpoint	Moira Stephen	0 7506 2420 5
Hard Drives	Ian Robertson	0 7506 2313 6
Windows 95	P.K. McBride	0 7506 2306 3
WordPro	Moira Stephen	0 7506 2626 7
Office 95	P.K. McBride	0 7506 2625 9

Office 95
Made Simple

P.K.McBride

MADE SIMPLE
BOOKS

Made Simple
An imprint of Butterworth-Heinemann Ltd
Linacre House, Jordan Hill, Oxford OX2 8DP

ℛ   A member of the Reed Elsevier plc group

OXFORD   LONDON   BOSTON
MUNICH   NEW DELHI   SINGAPORE   SYDNEY
TOKYO   TORONTO   WELLINGTON

First published 1996
© P K McBride 1996

TRADEMARKS/REGISTERED TRADEMARKS
Computer hardware and software brand names mentioned in this book are protected
by their respective trademarks and are acknowledged.

British Library Cataloguing in Publication Data
A catalogue record for this book is available from the British Library

ISBN 0 7506 2625 9

 Typeset by P.K.McBride, Southampton
Archtype, Bash Casual, Cotswold and Gravity fonts from Advanced Graphics Ltd
Icons designed by Sarah Ward © 1994
Printed and bound in Great Britain

Contents

Preface

This book is intended to be a companion to those others in this series that focus on individual Office applications – *Access*, *Excel*, *PowerPoint* and *Word Made Simple*.

Office 95 Made Simple concentrates on:

● the Office environment;

● those features and ways of working that are common to the applications;

● transferring and sharing data between applications, through copying, OLE (Object Linking and Embedding) , Binders and Mail Merge;

● the graphing and graphical add-ons that can be used within all applications;

● Schedule+, Office 95's personal (and workgroup) organiser.

The Office 95 suite contains so much, that it is not possible to cover it all in a book this size. I hope that I have included enough, and in enough detail, to give you what you need to get started and to work effectively across the applications.

To find out more about the individual components, see:

Access Made Simple by Moira Stephen

Excel Made Simple by Stephen Morris

PowerPoint Made Simple by Moira Stephen

Word Made Simple by Keith Brindley

1 Office management

The Office equipment

In the last few years Microsoft Office has established itself as the leading business application software suite. Office 95 is its successor, rewritten to take advantage of the greater speed and flexibility of Windows 95, and incorporating a new diary/organizer package.

The standard Office 95 suite contains:

 Word – a word processor that is extremely easy to use at a basic level, yet has all the features of a desktop publisher

 Excel – a spreadsheet that is powerful enough to handle the accounts of a multi-million pound company, yet simple enough for a child to use for a school project

 PowerPoint presentation software, for producing slideshows and accompanying handouts and notes

 Binder – a new concept and leap forward in integration. With the Binder you can store Word, Excel and Powerpoint documents in one file, and switch easily between them.

 Schedule+ is a diary, planner and address book. Networked users can share access to each other's planners, so that meetings can be arranged easily.

The hardware

Minimum requirements

Processor 486

RAM   8Mb

Hard disk 60Mb (free)

Monitor   VGA 800x640

Recommended

Processor Pentium

RAM   16Mb

Hard disk 80Mb (free)

Monitor   SVGA 1024x800

Take note

The main difference between Office 95 Pro and Standard is that the Professional edition also includes the Access database management software. Most of us will find that the combination of Excel and Mail Merge is enough for our data handling needs.

Minor applications

Take note

The Office package has an excellent 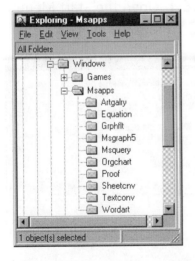 Help system, with the new Answer Wizard that understands (more or less) plain English.

Office 95 also has a large set of minor applications that are mainly run from within a major program. These can:

- add clip art (Artgalry), graphs (Msgraph5), equations, decorative text (Wordart) and charts (Orgchart) to Word or Powerpoint documents;

- convert spreadsheets (Sheetconv) and text files (Textconv) from one format to another;

- extract information from spreadsheets and databases (MSquery)

- display regional data on maps (Datamap)

- analyse your computer system (MSinfo)

Versions of most of these were present in the Windows 3.1 Office suite. Note that they were then stored in a directory called *Msapps*. Office 95 stores them in the *Common Files* folder. After installing Office 95 you may like to clear the *Msapps* files and free up some disk space.

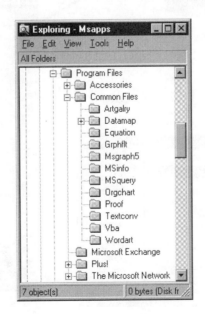

Your set of Common Files folders may differ from this – it depends upon which applications you chose to install. They can be added or removed at any time. (See page 12.)

As long as you are no longer using any Windows 3.1 versions of any Microsoft programs, you can delete all the Msapps folders.

Ready to start

There are several different ways to start the Office applications. Which one is best for you depends upon how you use them.

If you only use Office programs occasionally, you may as well work from the Start menu. With this approach it is worth adjusting the layout of items on the menu, through the **Settings** of the **Taskbar**. During installation all the applications, large and small, are placed in the Microsoft Office group – anything up to 20. This makes the menu hard to use. If you set up a sub-folder and push into it those that are rarely wanted, it will make life easier.

1 Click **Start**, point to **Settings** and select **Taskbar**

2 Click on the **Start Menu Programs** tab to open its panel

3 Click Advanced...

4 In Explorer, open the Programs folder and select **Microsoft Office**

5 Open the **File** menu, point to **New** and select **Folder**

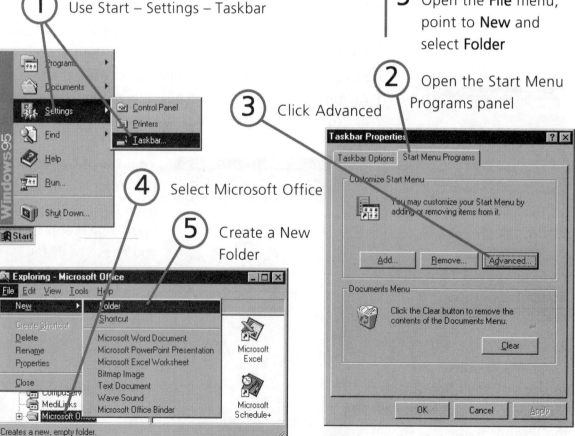

① Use Start – Settings – Taskbar

② Open the Start Menu Programs panel

③ Click Advanced

④ Select Microsoft Office

⑤ Create a New Folder

6 Rename the folder '*Accessories*'

7 Hold [Ctrl] and click on each of the items that to be moved

8 Keep the left button down and drag the selected items to Accessories

9 Close down Explorer and the Taskbar Properties box

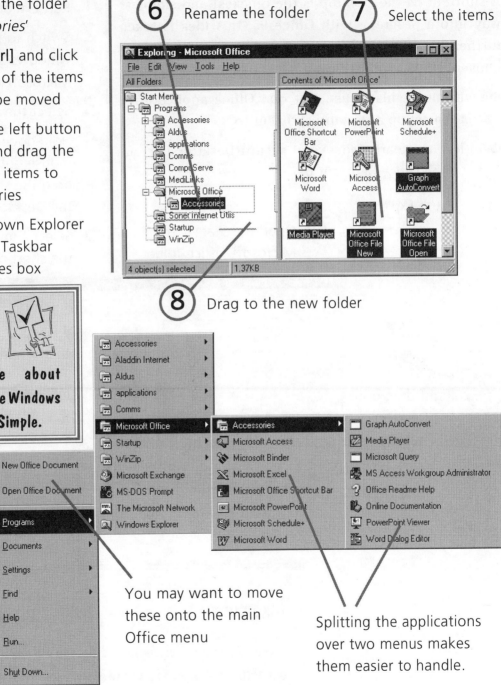

⑥ Rename the folder

⑦ Select the items

Exploring - Microsoft Office

File   Edit   View   Tools   Help

All Folders

- Start Menu
  - Programs
    - Accessories
    - Aldus
    - applications
    - Comms
    - CompuServe
    - MediLinks
    - Microsoft Office
      - Accessories
    - Sonet Internet Utils
    - Startup
    - WinZip

Contents of 'Microsoft Office'

Microsoft Office Shortcut Bar | Microsoft PowerPoint | Microsoft Schedule+

Microsoft Word | Microsoft Access | Graph AutoConvert

Media Player | Microsoft Office File New | Microsoft Office File Open

4 object(s) selected   1.37KB

⑧ Drag to the new folder

Tip

For more about menus, see Windows 95 Made Simple.

Accessories ▶
Aladdin Internet ▶
Aldus ▶
applications ▶
Comms ▶
Microsoft Office ▶
Startup ▶
WinZip ▶
Microsoft Exchange
MS-DOS Prompt
The Microsoft Network
Windows Explorer

Accessories ▶
Microsoft Access
Microsoft Binder
Microsoft Excel
Microsoft Office Shortcut Bar
Microsoft PowerPoint
Microsoft Schedule+
Microsoft Word

Graph AutoConvert
Media Player
Microsoft Query
MS Access Workgroup Administrator
Office Readme Help
Online Documentation
PowerPoint Viewer
Word Dialog Editor

New Office Document
Open Office Document
Programs ▶
Documents ▶
Settings ▶
Find ▶
Help
Run...
Shut Down...

Start

You may want to move these onto the main Office menu

Splitting the applications over two menus makes them easier to handle.

5

Office Shortcuts

A shortcut on the Desktop is the quickest and simplest way into a program. With Office 95, this idea is taken further in the Shortcut bar, giving instant access to your chosen Office applications.

- If you regularly use just one Office applications, then set up a Desktop shortcut to it.

- If you regularly use several, set up a Desktop shortcut to the Office Shortcut bar.

① Run Explorer

② Open the Start Menu/ Microsoft Office folder

④ Right-drag onto the Desktop

⑤ Select Copy Here

③ Select the shortcut

Take note

If you do a normal (left-button) drag, you will pull the shortcut out of the folder — and lose the entry from the Start menu.

The Shortcut Bar

❑ **Moving the Toolbar**

1 Point to an empty part of the bar

2 Drag to wherever you want it on the screen

To place it at the top, bottom or a side, push the cursor beyond the edge of the screen

By default, the Shortcut Bar sits at the top of the screen and contains buttons for opening or creating new files (of any Office sort), adding tasks, contacts or appointments to Schedule+ and for getting help. Its position and contents can be easily changed to suit your way of working.

The Bar can be a strip along any edge of the screen, or a compact block anywhere else. If it is on an edge, it can be set to Auto-hide. It will then shrink into the edge after use, and can be opened again by pointing into that edge.

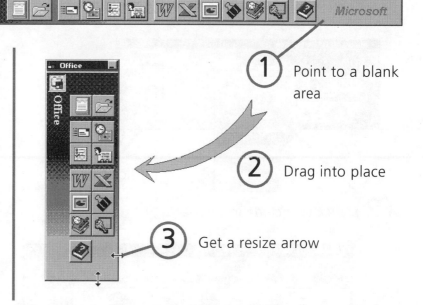

❑ **Adjusting the shape**

3 Move the cursor to an edge, to get the double-arrow cursor

4 Drag to resize

❑ **Setting Auto-Hide**

5 Click the square at the top left of the Toolbar to open the menu

6 Click to turn **Auto Hide** on ✓ or off

① Point to a blank area

② Drag into place

③ Get a resize arrow

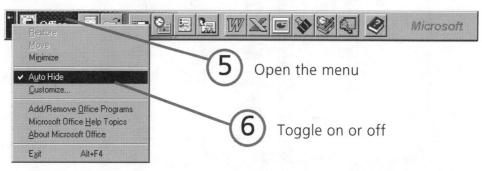

⑤ Open the menu

⑥ Toggle on or off

Multiple bars

An Office toolbar represents a folder. Its shortcuts, programs and sub-folders become items on the bar. If you are interested, the main Toolbar is the folder */MSOffice/ Office/Shortcut Bar/Office*. Use Explorer or My Computer to look in there and you will see that each button is an item in the folder.

If you like the toolbar approach, you can add toolbars for other folders to the Shortcut Bar, so that you can run programs from here, as well as from the Desktop and/or Start menu.

❑ **Adding Toolbars**

1 Right click in a clear part of the Toolbar, to get the short menu

2 Click to add ✓ a toolbar to the list

❑ You can only see the buttons of one toolbar at a time. Click on a compressed bar to open it up.

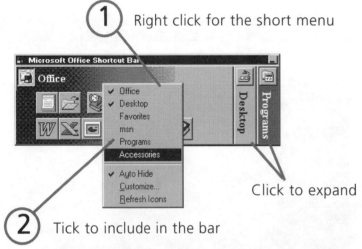

Right click for the short menu

Click to expand

Tick to include in the bar

Take note

If you want to add a folder to the toolbar that it not in the list on the short menu, use the Toolbars panel in the Customize dialog box. (See the next page.)

The shortcuts in this folder can become buttons on the Office Toolbar

Basic steps

1 Right click on the Toolbar to open the short menu

2 Select **Customize**

3 Open the **Buttons** panel

4 Pick a **Toolbar**

5 Click the □ to add ✓ or remove □ a button

6 Click **OK**

Customising Shortcut bars

The most useful change you can make to the Shortcut Toolbar is adjusting its contents so that you have buttons for the applications that you use – and no others cluttering it up. But you can also tailor its appearance, and you should check the Settings as this tells Office where to look for Templates.

● As well as adding shortcuts from the Office set, you can also add a link to any other program on your system, or to a folder – these buttons open a My Computer display for the folder.

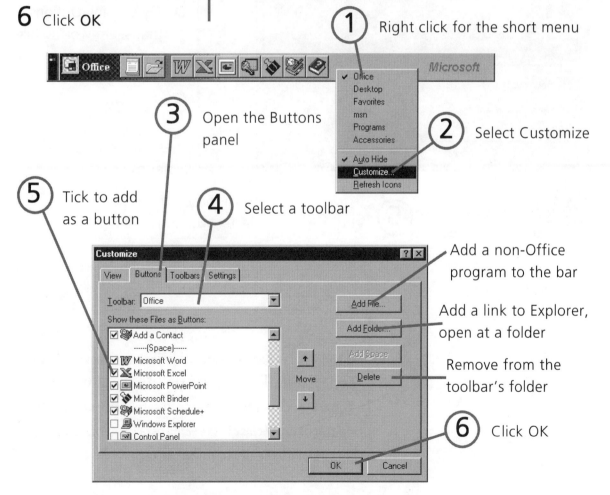

① Right click for the short menu

③ Open the Buttons panel

② Select Customize

⑤ Tick to add as a button

④ Select a toolbar

Add a non-Office program to the bar

Add a link to Explorer, open at a folder

Remove from the toolbar's folder

⑥ Click OK

Changing views

You can change the colour, button size and other aspects of the Toolbar displays, using the View panel.

The Options apply to all toolbars, though the Colour choices only apply to the selected toolbar.

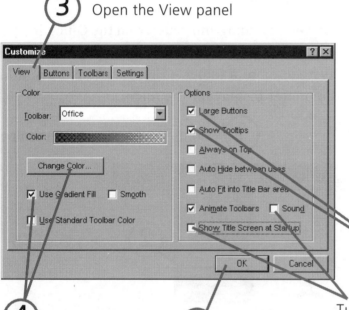

③ Open the View panel

④ Set the colour for the selected bar

⑥ Click OK

These make Toolbars easier to use

Turn these off for faster working

Basic steps

1 Right click on the Toolbar to open the short menu

2 Select **Customize**

3 Open the **View** panel

4 In the **Colors** pane, select the **Toolbar** then pick the **Color** and **Fill** style

5 Try out any **Options** that seem worthwhile – you can always reset them again

6 Click **OK**

Tip

If you want to use the Auto-Hide feature, you may find it best to locate the Toolbar on the left edge of the screen. You are less likely to activate accidentally there than at the right or bottom (close to the scroll bars) or at the top (close to the menu bar and control buttons).

Basic steps

1 Open the **Customize** dialog box if necessary

2 Click **Settings** to open its panel

3 Select an **Item** if you think its **Setting** is wrong

4 Click Modify...

5 Either type in the correct path to the folder, or Browse... to locate it.

6 Click **OK** to fix the new setting.

At some point before you start to use Templates, you should check the Settings panel to make sure that Office 95 is using the right folders.

It normally assumes that the ready-made templates and those that you build yourself will all be stored in the *C:\MSOffice\Templates* folder. If you have created a new folder for your templates, or placed the ready-made ones elsewhere, the Settings should be adjusted to match.

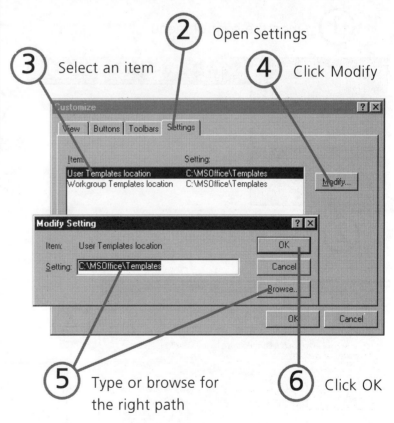

② Open Settings

③ Select an item

④ Click Modify

⑤ Type or browse for the right path

⑥ Click OK

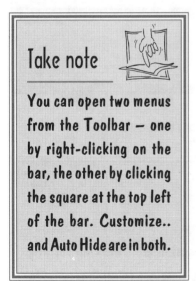

Take note

You can open two menus from the Toolbar – one by right-clicking on the bar, the other by clicking the square at the top left of the bar. Customize.. and Auto Hide are in both.

Add/remove programs

After you have been using Office for a little while, you may decide that there some applications that you do not use, and which should be removed to free up space, or others which you did not install initially, but which you would now like to try.

The Setup and Uninstall routine provides a simple way to add or remove programs. It can be reached through the Shortcut bar or through the Windows 95 Control Panel.

1 Click the square at the top left of the bar to get the control menu

2 Select **Add/Remove Programs**

3 At the **Office Setup** panel, select **Office 95** and click **OK**

4 At the main **Setup** panel, click Add/Remove...

① Open the control menu

② Select Add/Remove Programs

③ Click Office 95 and OK

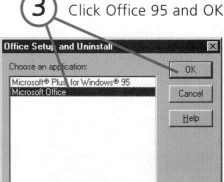

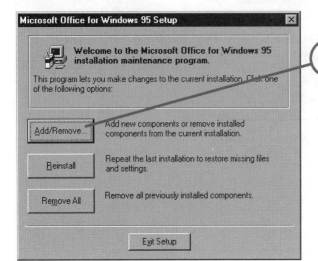

④ Click Add/Remove

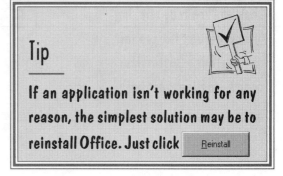

Tip

If an application isn't working for any reason, the simplest solution may be to reinstall Office. Just click Reinstall

Selective installations

5 Select an item from the Options list

6 Click [Change Option...] to select elements to add or remove

7 At the next level, if you select an item and [Change Option...] is active, click it to select from its sub-set

8 Set a tick by the elements you want to include, or remove the tick from those you want to uninstall

9 Click **OK**

Each entry in the main Options list – and some in the second level of lists – represents a set of programs. If the box is grey, only some are installed. The Change Option button lets you select the elements you want to include.

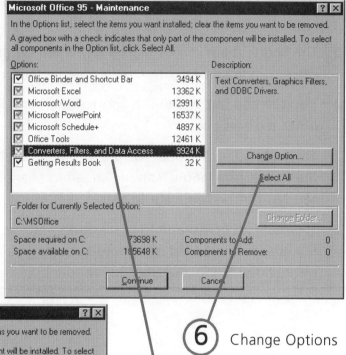

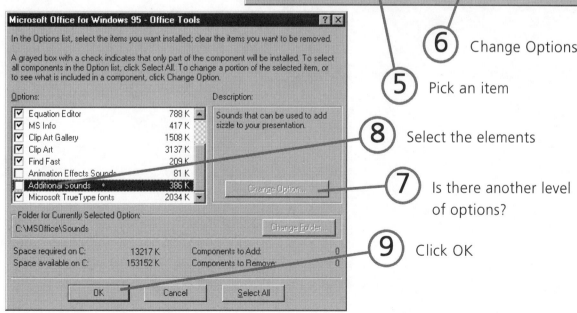

6 Change Options

5 Pick an item

8 Select the elements

7 Is there another level of options?

9 Click OK

Summary

- The **Office 95 suite** contains four (or five) major applications, plus many utilities that can be used from within the main applications.

- Office programs can be run from the **Start menu, Desktop shortcuts** or the **Shortcut Bar** – pick the approach that best suits your way of working.

- The **Shortcut Bar** can be placed anywhere on the screen, and can be set to hideitself when not in use.

- You can **add buttons** to the Shortcut Bar, and **link other toolbars** onto it.

- The **Settings panel** contains core information about the Office installation. You may need to change settings for the **Template folders**.

- The main programs and their many optional features can be **added or removed** at any time through the Setup and Uninstall routines.

2 Help!

Starting Help

There are six aspects to Help in the Office 95 applications:

- an organised **Contents** list;
- **Index**ed Help pages;
- a word-based **Find** facility;
- the Answer Wizard;
- point and click help;
- the Tip Wizard.

The first four form the main Help system.

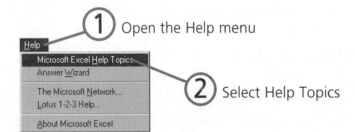

① Open the Help menu

② Select Help Topics

Tip

You can press [F1] — anywhere, any time — to get into the Help system.

Tips

Every time you start up – until you turn the feature off – you get a Tip of the Day. The tips are chosen at random, but can be a painless way to widen your understanding of the applications.

Within the applications, if you click 💡 you will get a tip that is related to the last job you did – or the last error report that came up. These are stored in the Tip Wizard toolbar, and can be scrolled back through, if necessary.

The Tip toolbar is normally slotted into the top frame. This one has been floated free to show the title.

Scroll through past tips

TipWizard ❌
💡 3) To move a docked toolbar to the last floating position it occupied, double-click the toolbar background. Double-click again to return it to the last docked position.

Basic steps

1 Click the **Contents** tab if this panel is not at the front already.

2 Point to ● and click ▭ **Open** to see the page titles.

3 Point to ? and click ▭ **Display** to read the page.

either

4 Click **Help Topics** to return to the Contents panel

or

5 Click ✕ to close the page and exit Help

Contents

This approach treats the Help pages as a book. You scan through the headings to find a section that seems to cover what you want, and open that to see the page titles. (Some sections have sub-sections, making it a 2 or 3 stage process to get to page titles.)

Some Help topics are stand alone pages; others have **Related topics** buttons to take you on to further pages.

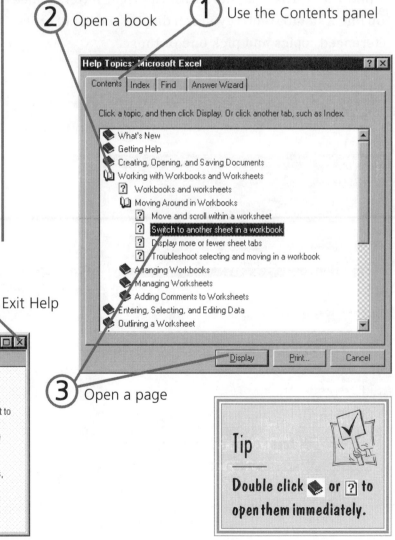

② Open a book   ① Use the Contents panel

Help Topics: Microsoft Excel   ? ✕

Contents | Index | Find | Answer Wizard

Click a topic, and then click Display. Or click another tab, such as Index.

- ● What's New
- ● Getting Help
- ● Creating, Opening, and Saving Documents
- 📖 Working with Workbooks and Worksheets
    - ? Workbooks and worksheets
    - 📖 Moving Around in Workbooks
        - ? Move and scroll within a worksheet
        - ? Switch to another sheet in a workbook
        - ? Display more or fewer sheet tabs
        - ? Troubleshoot selecting and moving in a workbook
- ● Arranging Workbooks
- ● Managing Worksheets
- ● Adding Comments to Worksheets
- ● Entering, Selecting, and Editing Data
- ● Outlining a Worksheet

Display | Print... | Cancel

④ Go back for more

⑤ Exit Help

③ Open a page

? Microsoft Excel   _ □ ✕

Help Topics | Back | Options

Switch to another sheet in a workbook

- Click the sheet tab for the sheet you want to work on.

    If you don't see the tab you want, click the tab scrolling buttons to display the tab. Then click the tab.

Tip If your workbook contains many sheets, use the right mouse button to click the tab scrolling buttons. Then click the sheet you want.

Tip

Double click ● or ? to open them immediately.

17

Using the Index

Though the Contents are good for getting an overview of how things work, if you want help on a specific problem – usually the case – you are better off with the Index.

This is organised through a cross-referenced list of terms. The main list is alphabetical, with sub-entries, just like the index in a book. And, as with an index in a book, you can plough through it slowly from the top, or skip through to find the words that start with the right letters. Once you find a suitable entry, you can display the list of cross-referenced topics and pick one of those.

Basic steps

1 Click the **Index** tab

2 Start to type a word into the slot to focus the entries list or use the scroll bar to find the topic

3 Select the entry

4 Click [Display]

Take note

If there is only one relevant topic page, the system will take you directly to it after Step 4.

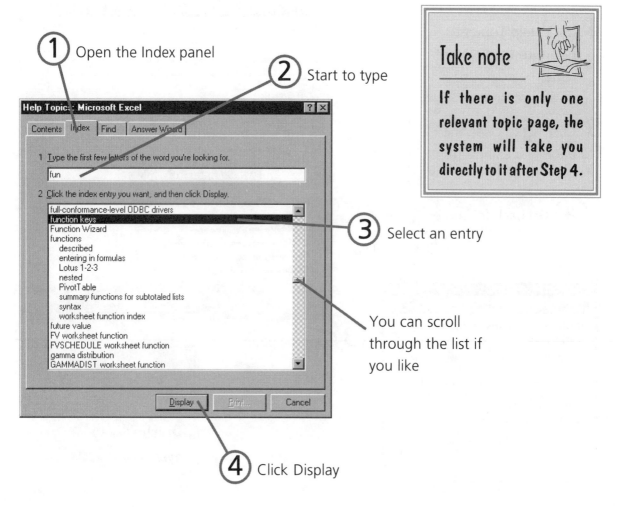

① Open the Index panel

② Start to type

③ Select an entry

You can scroll through the list if you like

④ Click Display

5 Pick the most suitable topic from the **Topics Found** list

6 Click [Display]

☐ The help page will open. When you have done with it you can click **Help Topics** to return to the Index or ⊠ to close the page and exit Help

☐ **Point and click help**

1 Click on ? or ▶?

2 Click the ▶? cursor on the item that you want to know about.

3 After you have read the help box, click anywhere to close it.

⑤ Pick a topic

If you cannot see anything useful, close the panel and return to the Index

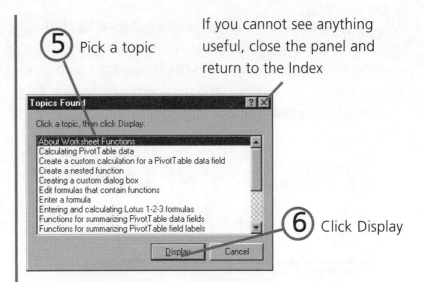

⑥ Click Display

The query icon

All the dialog boxes and panels have ? on the top right of the title bar. You will also find ▶? on some toolbars. Use them to learn more about objects on screen.

① Click the query icon

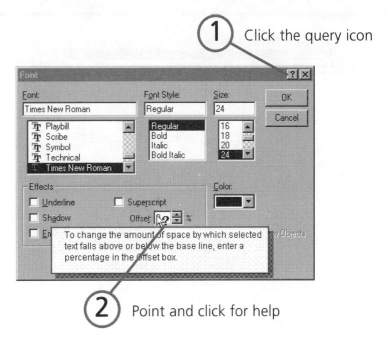

To change the amount of space by which selected text falls above or below the base line, enter a percentage in the Offset box.

② Point and click for help

Finding help

If you can't track down the help you need from the Index, you can **Find** it using the third Help panel. This works by creating a list of all the words in the Help pages; you give it one or more words to search for and it produces a list of all the topics that contain matching words.

1 Open the **Find** panel in **Help Topics**

2 Type your word into the top slot. As you type, words starting with the typed letters appear in the pane beneath.

3 If you want to narrow the search, go back to step 2, type a space after your first word and give another.

4 Select the most suitable word from the **Narrow the search** pane

5 Select a topic from the lower pane

6 Click [Display]

Use Clear if you want to start a new search

(2) Type a word

(1) Click Find

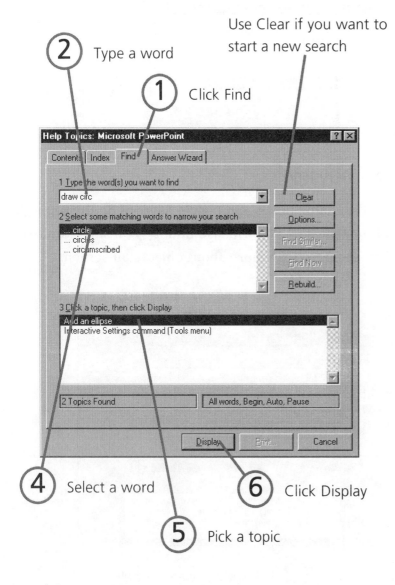

(4) Select a word

(5) Pick a topic

(6) Click Display

Tip

If you want to have the Help page in sight, right click on it, to open its short menu and turn on **Keep Help on Top.**

Basic steps

❑ **Narrowing the scope**

1 On the **Find** panel, click
  [Options...]

2 On the **Find Options**
  panel, click [Files...]

❑ This shows a list of the
  Help files that will be
  searched. Some of
  these are not relevant

3 Hold **[Ctrl]** and click on
  the files that you want
  it to ignore. If you
  remove one by
  mistake, click again to
  reselect it

4 Click **OK** then close the
  Options panel.

Take note

**The first time you use
Find for any application,
a Wizard will run to create
the word list. Take the
Minimum option – it is
quicker and should do all
you want.**

Find options

There are several Options that you can set to alter the
nature of the search or narrow its scope.

In the **Search for words containing** box, select

All the words.. where you are using several words to
focus on one topic

At least one.. where you are giving several alternatives in
the hope that it recognises one

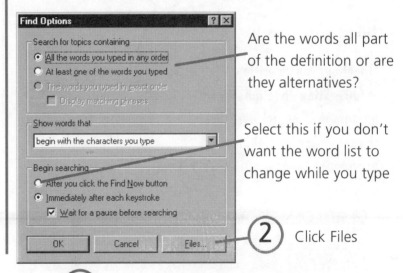

Are the words all part
of the definition or are
they alternatives?

Select this if you don't
want the word list to
change while you type

② Click Files

③ [Ctrl] and click to remove or reselect

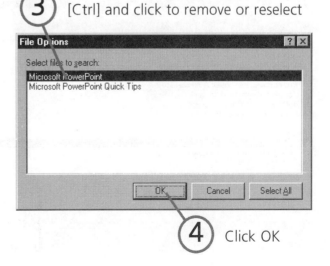

④ Click OK

Answer Wizard

The Answer Wizard is designed to make help even more accessible by answering questions written in plain English. It usually offers two sets of help pages:

● How Do I – standard help pages

● Tell Me About – pages with a friendlier tip-based approach.

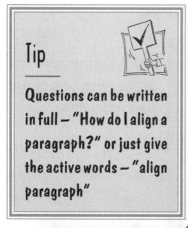

Tip

Questions can be written in full – "How do I align a paragraph?" or just give the active words – "align paragraph"

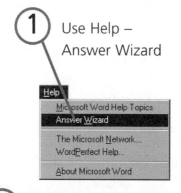

① Use Help – Answer Wizard

② Enter the question

Basic steps

1 Pull down the **Help** menu and select **Answer Wizard**

2 Type your question into the top slot

3 Click [Search]

4 Select a topic from the list and click [Display]

5 On **Tell Me About** pages, click on a heading to display its brief help.

6 Return to **Help topics** or click [x] to exit

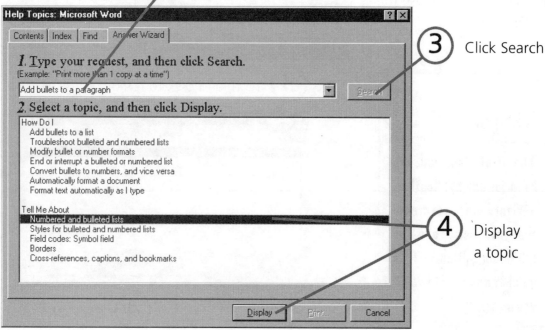

③ Click Search

④ Display a topic

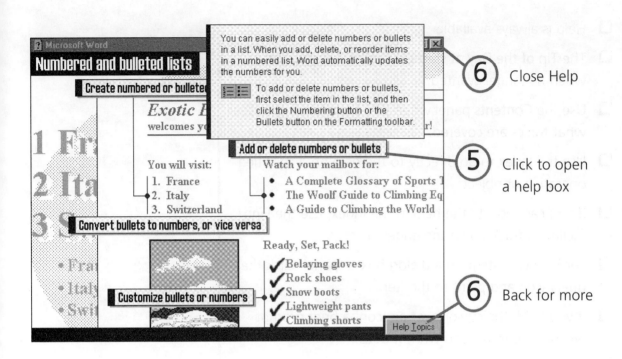

You can easily add or delete numbers or bullets in a list. When you add, delete, or reorder items in a numbered list, Word automatically updates the numbers for you.

To add or delete numbers or bullets, first select the item in the list, and then click the Numbering button or the Bullets button on the Formatting toolbar.

6 Close Help

5 Click to open a help box

6 Back for more

Past questions are stored. To return to a topic, drop down the list and select from there.

Take note

Answer Wizard is not perfect. Sometimes you have to ask the same question in several ways before you get a useful help topic.

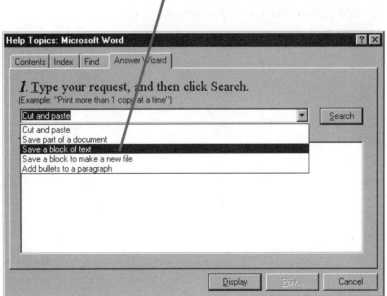

Summary

❑ Help is always available.

❑ The **Tip of the Day** at start up can be switched off when no longer wanted.

❑ Use the **Contents** panel when you are browsing to see what topics are covered.

❑ Use the **Index** to go directly to the help on a specified operation or object.

❑ If you can't locate the help in the Index, use the **Find** facility to track down the pages.

❑ For help with items in a **dialog box** or **panel**, click the query icon and point to the item.

❑ If you hold the cursor over an **icon**, a brief prompt will pop up to tell you what it does.

❑ The **Answer Wizard** can handle questions written in simple English.

❑ The **Tell Me About** help pages contain a set of related tips rather than a single item of text.

3 Common features

Menus and toolbars

The Office 95 suite is a huge and complex piece of software, yet it is very straightforward to use – at a basic level. (It takes time and effort to master all of its intricacies!) One of the key factors in this ease of use is that – wherever possible – the same jobs are performed using the same commands, accessed from the same buttons or menus, in all applications. As the applications share a large core of common tasks, once you have got the hang of one application, you are on the way to mastering the next.

Menus

Commands are grouped sensibly on the menus. Browse through them and you will quickly get a sense of the type of command to be found on each menu.

If a menu item is followed by ... then selecting it opens up a dialog box or options panel where you specify details.

❑ Using menus

1 Click on a name or hold down [Alt] and press the underlined letter (usually the first) in the name to drop down its menu

2 Point and click to select a menu item

or

3 Use the [Up] and [Down] arrow keys to highlight a menu item, then press [Enter]

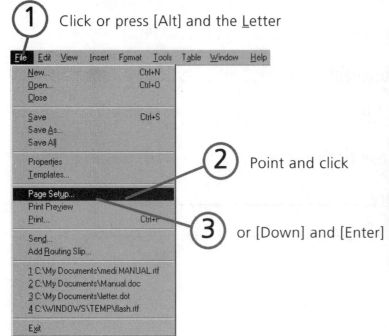

① Click or press [Alt] and the Letter

② Point and click

③ or [Down] and [Enter]

Tip

When a menu is open, you can switch to another by pointing at the name in the menu bar, or by pressing the [Left] and [Right] arrow keys.

Toolbars

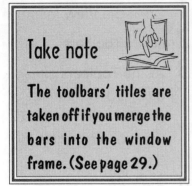

Take note

The toolbars' titles are taken off if you merge the bars into the window frame. (See page 29.)

The buttons on the toolbars give quick and easy access to the more commonly used commands. Each application has half a dozen or more toolbars, four of which – with variations – are found in all.

Some toolbars are open by default, but all can be displayed or removed as required. You can also add or remove buttons from any bar. Both of these aspects are covered on the next page.

The **Standard** toolbars from Word (top), Excel (middle) and PowerPoint (bottom). These hold the buttons for most commonly used commands – for file handling, printing, editing, zooming (screen magnification) and help.

Note how many of the same buttons are present on all three toolbars.

Word, Excel and PowerPoint all have these toolbars, though their contents vary slightly.

Formatting sets the style, alignment and layout of text.

Drawing has line and shape tools for creating diagrams.

The **Microsoft** toolbar gives you yet another way to run Microsoft applications – and you get the buttons whether or not you have the software!

27

Selecting toolbars

If you find toolbars useful – and you will – you can have more on screen than just the default ones. But don't overdo it. Every toolbar you add reduces the amount of visible working space!

Basic steps

1 Open the **View** menu

2 Select **Toolbars...**

3 At the **Toolbars** dialog box, click on a name to add ✓ or remove ☐ the toolbar from the screen

4 Click **OK**

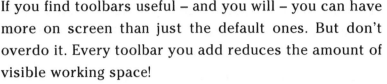

① Open the View menu

② Select Toolbars

③ Click to turn the display on or off

④ Click OK to exit

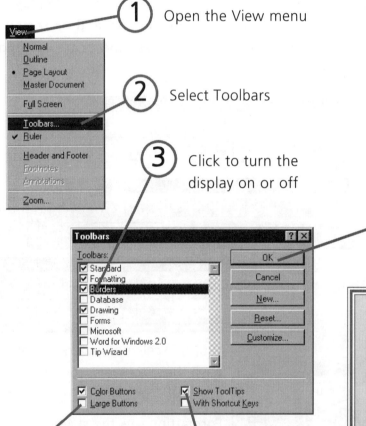

Large buttons are easier to identify, but take up more space.

Tool tips remind you what the buttons do. Pause the cursor over a button to see its tip.

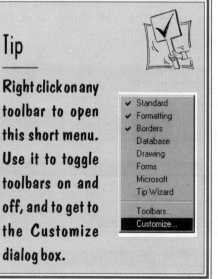

Tip

Right click on any toolbar to open this short menu. Use it to toggle toolbars on and off, and to get to the Customize dialog box.

28

Basic steps

1 Point to the title bar (if visible) or any blank area of the toolbar

2 Drag the outline, pushing it off the edge if you want to merge it into the frame.

3 Release the mouse button to drop into place.

Placing toolbars

Button toolbars can be merged into the window frame, or allowed to 'float' on the document area. The position and size of floating toolbars can be adjusted at any time.

Those bars that you want to use all of the time are probably best fitted into the frame. Those that are only wanted for the occasional job – e.g. Drawing for creating an illustration – can be brought up as needed, and floated in a convenient place.

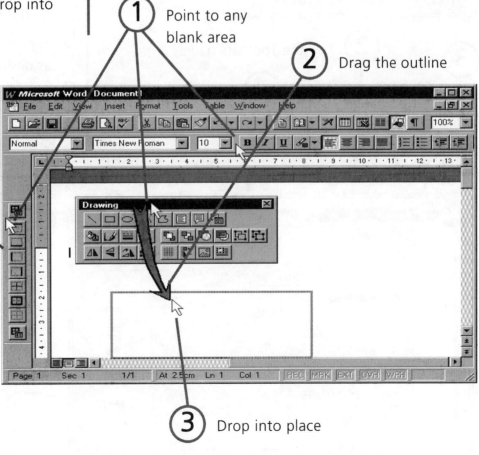

① Point to any blank area

② Drag the outline

You can drag bars within the frame, if needed

③ Drop into place

Adding and removing buttons

You can add buttons to, or remove them from, a toolbar that is on display on screen. New buttons can be from any category, though it helps to keep the same kind together.

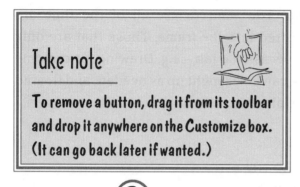

Take note

To remove a button, drag it from its toolbar and drop it anywhere on the Customize box. (It can go back later if wanted.)

1 Right click a toolbar for the short menu and select **Customize..**

2 Open the **Toolbars** panel

3 Select the **Category**

4 Drag the required button onto the main window and drop it on the target toolbar.

5 Repeat steps 3 and 4 as desired

6 Click **Close**

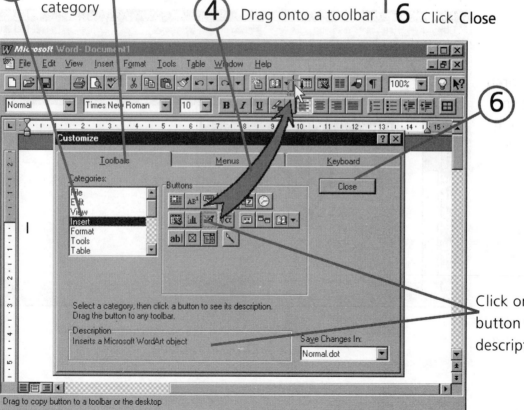

③ Select a category

② Use the Toolbars panel

④ Drag onto a toolbar

⑥ Close

Click on a button for its description

Basic steps

1 Right click a toolbar for the short menu and select **Customize..**

2 Open the **Menus** panel

3 Select the **Category**

4 Scroll through the **Commands** and highlight the one you want to add

5 Drop down the **Position on menu** list and highlight the item *below* which the new one will go

6 Click [Add Below]

7 Click [Close]

Customizing menus is a job that you will not want to get into straight away, but it is useful to know that is can be done – easily. You might, for instance, find that you often use Word Art to decorate PowerPoint documents. An *Insert Word Art* menu item would simplify this.

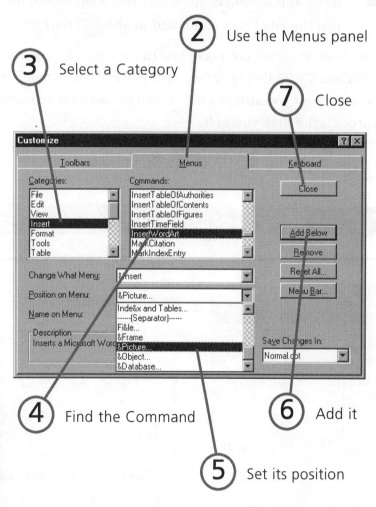

② Use the Menus panel

③ Select a Category

⑦ Close

④ Find the Command

⑥ Add it

⑤ Set its position

Tip

Those commands that you do not use can be removed from menus, making them easier to work with. Don't worry about making a mess of your menus – the Reset All button will put things back to normal.

Opening files

There are several ways to open an existing Office file. Which way to take depends largely upon where you are when you start:

- If you have not yet opened the application, use , the File Open shortcut, on the Office Shortcut bar.

- If the application is open, but you want an old file, use the File Open command or the button.

The first two ways both take you to the Open dialog box. This has file finding facilities, so if you cannot remember which folder you stored a file in, you do not have to trawl through the disk yourself.

① Click the Open button

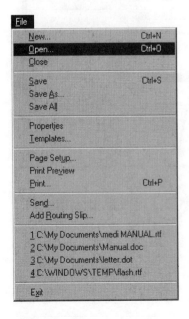

1 Click on the Toolbar or on the Shortcut bar

2 **Look in** the folder where the file is

3 If you want to reduce the file list then..

4 Set the **Files of type** to the appropriate type

5 Drop down the **Last modified** list and set the timescale

6 Click on possible files and use for the **Preview** or for the **Properties** view to check them out

7 When you can see the file you want, select it and click Open

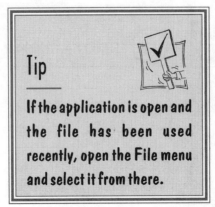

Tip

If the application is open and the file has been used recently, open the File menu and select it from there.

32

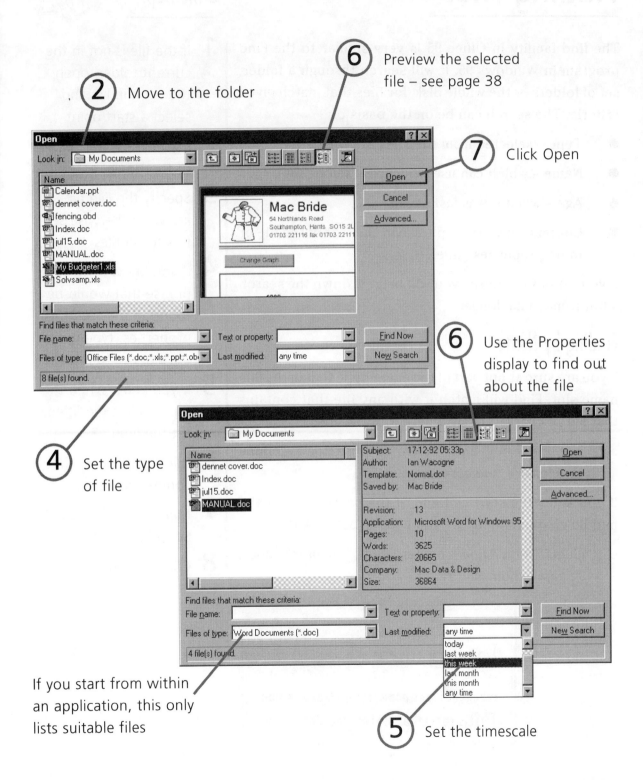

(6) Preview the selected file – see page 38

(2) Move to the folder

(7) Click Open

(6) Use the Properties display to find out about the file

(4) Set the type of file

If you start from within an application, this only lists suitable files

(5) Set the timescale

Finding files

The find facility in Office 95 is very similar to the Find program in Windows 95. It will search through a folder, set of folders or the whole disk, for files that match given criteria. The search can be on the basis of:

● **Type** – selected from the Files of type list

● **Name** – which can use wildcards (see below)

● **Age** – when it was last saved

● **Content** – a word or phrase in the text of the file or in its properties panel

If you set more criteria, you will narrow down the search – but it may take longer.

Finding by Name

If you are sure about part of the name, type that in the File name slot. Find will match it with any file that contains that set of characters anywhere in the name:

e.g. *"memo"* would find *"memo* to boss.doc", "29june *memo*.txt", "*memo*ry costs.xls"

If you know the start and end of the name, but not the middle characters, fill the gap with an asterisk (*):

e.g. *"chap*2"* would find *"chap*ter*2*.doc", "*chap*ter*20*.doc", "*chap*el choir may 1*2*.txt"

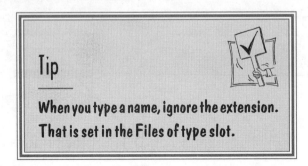

Tip

When you type a name, ignore the extension. That is set in the Files of type slot.

1 If the file is not in the current folder, open the Look in list and select a start point

2 If you know part or all of the Name, enter it

3 Specify the File type if known, otherwise set this to All files

4 If you know a word or phrase that would be found in the file or its properties, type it into the slot, in "quotes"

5 If you know when the file was last modified, set the limit

6 Click 🔲 to open the commands menu

7 Make sure that **Search Subfolders** is on ✓

8 Click Find Now

Take note

The Look in list lets you move to another drive or to the folder above the current one. To select another folder, go up to Drive C: then double click on the folder in the Name list.

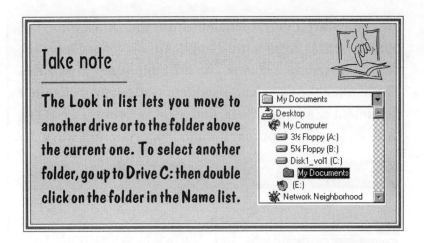

① Set where to start looking

Shortcut to the Favorites folder

⑦ Search Subfolders

⑥ Open the menu

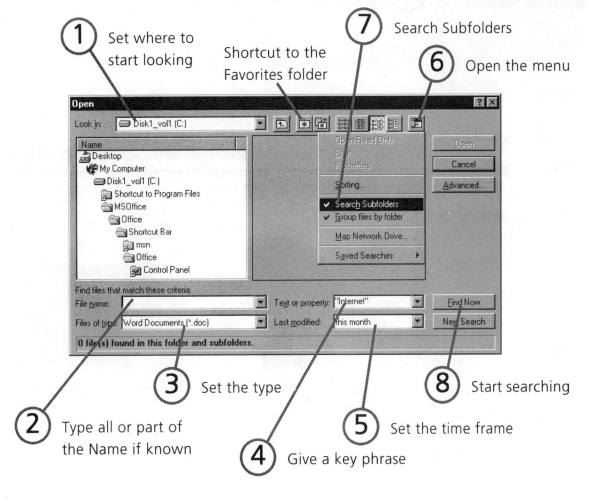

③ Set the type

② Type all or part of the Name if known

④ Give a key phrase

⑤ Set the time frame

⑧ Start searching

New documents

You can start a new document from the Office Shortcut bar as well as from within applications. The document can be based on a 'blank', or on a template or wizard. These offer the same end-products – attractive, effective documents, spreadsheets and presentations, for very little effort – but approach them from different ways.

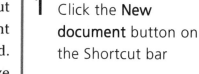

① Click New Document

② Use File – New

The Previews are small but useful

③ Open the panel

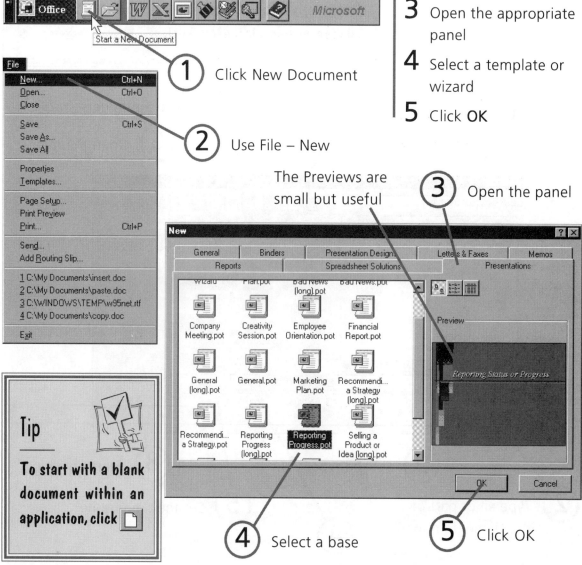

Tip

To start with a blank document within an application, click 🗋

④ Select a base

⑤ Click OK

36

Templates and Wizards

Fonts, styles and layouts are already in place

Templates are designed and formatted layouts with 'Click here to enter...' prompts wherever your own data is needed; Excel templates also have appropriate headings and formulae.

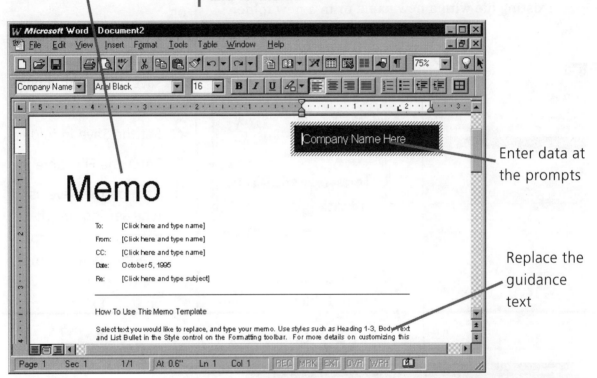

Enter data at the prompts

Replace the guidance text

Wizards collect data and option choices from you, through a series of dialog boxes, then generate a formatted document. Like a template, this will have formulae and 'Click here to enter...' prompts, but will also incorporate your data and have been customised to suit your option choices.

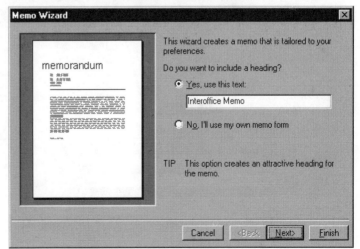

Saving files

There are two file saving routines in Office applications.

- **Save** is used to save an existing file after editing

- **Save As** is used to save a new file, or to save an existing file with a new name or in a new folder.

Basic steps

- **Save As**

1 Click 💾 to save a new file

or

1 Open the **File** menu and select **Save As** to save a file with a new name or location

2 Set the **Save in** folder

3 Enter the **Filename**

4 Change the **Save as type** setting only if you do not want to use the native format – e.g. not *doc* in Word or *xls* in Excel

5 Click 　Save

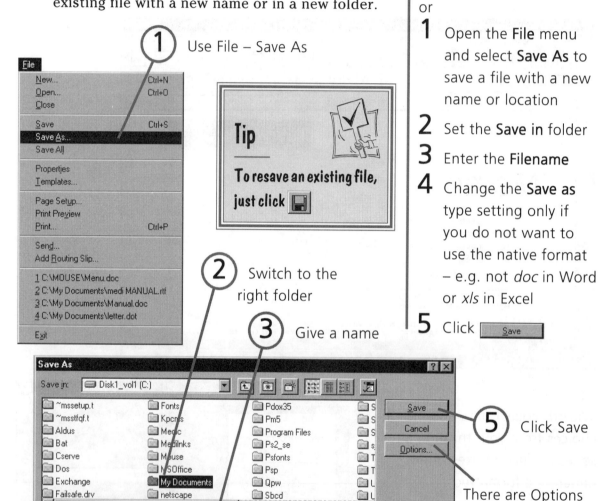

Use File – Save As

Tip

To resave an existing file, just click 💾

② Switch to the right folder

③ Give a name

⑤ Click Save

There are Options – see opposite

④ Set the type if different

38

Save options

These vary between the applications. Word has an extensive Options panel, Excel has a simpler one, and Powerpoint has a single option, in the Save dialog box!

Word and Excel offer three levels of protection:

With a **protection password**, the document cannot be opened without the password

Write reservation allows anyone to read it, but only the password holder can save it, with the same name

Read recommended sets no password, but does not allow the file to be saved, except with a new name

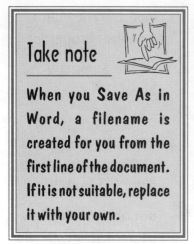
If you have any doubts about the PC's reliability, turn on the **Always create Backup** option

PowerPoint also lets you **Embed True Type fonts**, to ensure that the document looks the same on any PC.

Automatic save guards against lost work – but set it to a reasonable interval

Word

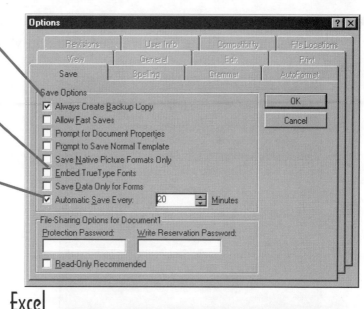

Excel

File properties

When looking at the File Find facility, we saw that you can check the nature of a file by reading its Properties panels.

● The **General** panel holds the basic details of the file – location, size, date saved, etc.

● The **Statistics** panel (below) has a more complete set of figures – the Word Count is useful for students, journalists or anyone else working to a set limit.

● Some of the information on the **Summary** panel (opposite) is produced by Office 95; some you have to supply yourself.

● The **Contents** can be used to list the titles of slides in a presentation, or sheets in an Excel book.

● The **Custom** panel can hold details of fields within the document – this is for advanced users only!

Basic steps

1 Open the **File** menu and select **Properties**

2 Use the **Summary** panel

3 Enter information as required – the **Subject** and **Keywords** will be useful in future Finds

4 Turn on **Save Preview Picture** if this will help to identify the file later – it's not much use with simple text!

5 Click **OK**

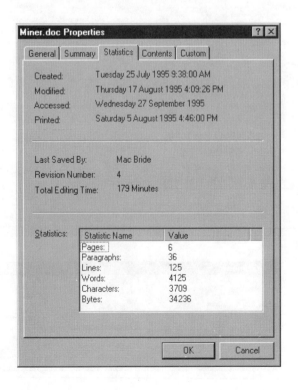

Miner.doc Properties

General | Summary | Statistics | Contents | Custom

Created:	Tuesday 25 July 1995 9:38:00 AM
Modified:	Thursday 17 August 1995 4:09:26 PM
Accessed:	Wednesday 27 September 1995
Printed:	Saturday 5 August 1995 4:46:00 PM

Last Saved By:	Mac Bride
Revision Number:	4
Total Editing Time:	179 Minutes

Statistics:

Statistic Name	Value
Pages:	6
Paragraphs:	36
Lines:	125
Words:	4125
Characters:	3709
Bytes:	34236

OK | Cancel

Take note

The General, Summary and Statistics panels can also be opened from within Explorer, but Contents and Custom are only accessible from within the Office filing routines.

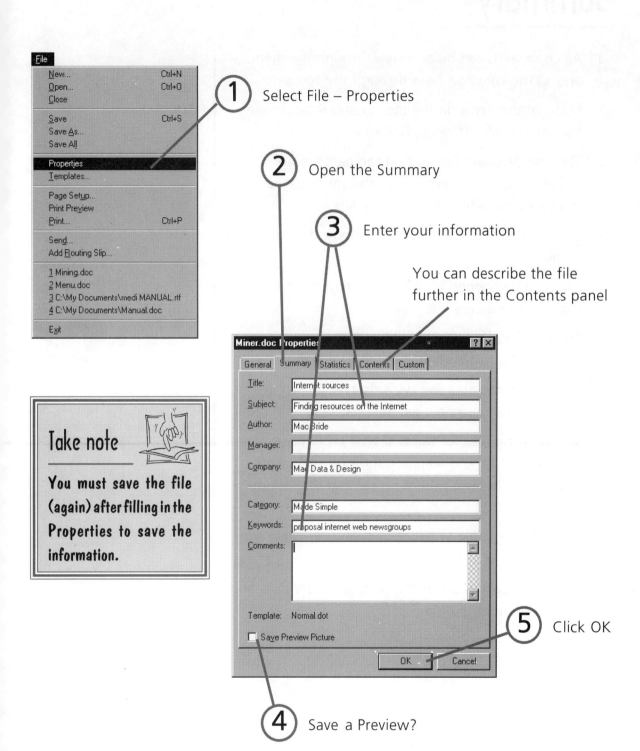

① Select File – Properties

② Open the Summary

③ Enter your information

You can describe the file further in the Contents panel

Take note

You must save the file (again) after filling in the Properties to save the information.

⑤ Click OK

④ Save a Preview?

41

Summary

- All commands can be accessed through the menus, and all the common ones through the toolbars

- Many of the items on the menus and toolbars are the same in all Office applications.

- The **Standard** and **Formatting toolbars** are normally displayed. Other ones can be brought onto the screen as and when they are needed.

- Commands can be **added to** or **removed from** your menus

- **Files can be opened** from the Shortcut bar or from within applications.

- The **File Find** facility helps you to track down files if you have forgotten their names or folders.

- There are **templates** and **wizards** available to simplify setting up new documents.

- When **saving files** for the first time, you must specify a folder and filename through the Save As dialog box. Resaving them simply takes a click on the Save button

- When saving a file, if you also save its **Preview**, you may make it easier to identify it in future.

- A file's **Properties** panel can hold summary data and a description of the file.

4 Outputs

Printing

Because of their different natures, the Office applications have significant differences in their printing routines.

● Word documents are page-based from the start, leading to a simple transition from screen to paper.

● Excel spreadsheets are of indefinite size and highly variable layout. The printout may fit on a single page or be spread across many. To get a good-looking printout you may have to adjust the orientation of the paper, the scale of the print, the output sequence and other aspects.

● PowerPoint is based around slides, and works to fairly formal layouts. This leaves little room for variation in output either to slides or to paper.

Despite the differences, there remain many similarities, particularly between Excel and Word.

Excel

❑ **Instant print**
1 Check the printer is on
2 Click 🖶

❑ **Controlled printing**
1 Check the printer
2 In Excel, use **File – Print Area** to select the block of cells to print
3 Open the **File** menu and select **Print**
4 Change the **Printer Name** if necessary
5 In PowerPoint and Word, set the **range** of pages or slides to print
6 Set the number of copies
7 Click **OK**

③ Select the printer

④ Print part or all

⑥ How many copies

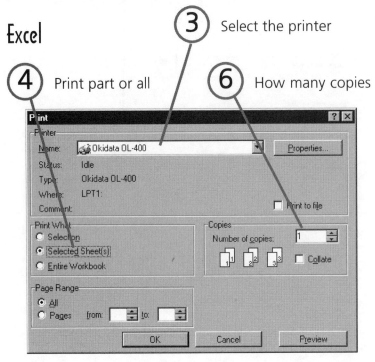

Take note

If you click 🖶 it sends the document to the printer directly, without giving you the chance to adjust the settings

PowerPoint

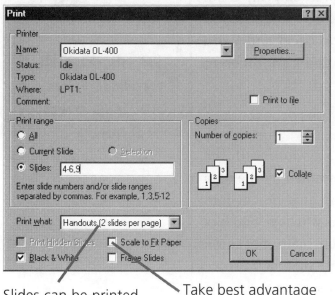

Slides can be printed
in different ways

Take best advantage
of the paper

Tip

Click the Properties button to set the paper-handling, dots per inch resolution, and other aspects of the printer.

Word

A Word document has many additional parts, some of which are only of interest to its author

Take note

If you are printing multiple copies, turning on the Collate option will save you sorting the pages, but can make printing much slower as each copiy has to be output separately.

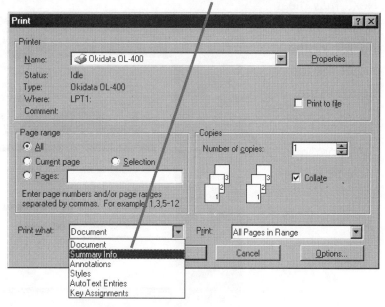

Print Preview

The Preview routines are there not just so that you can *see* how the whole document will look when printed out on separate sheets of paper. They are also there so that you can *change* how it will look. The Excel and Word preview tools are different because there are different kinds of adjustments to make.

Excel

Spreadsheets are usually designed as a whole with the layout and size of blocks of data determined by the data itself. To output them to paper, they must be cut into sections. The odds are that some pages will have odd bits of data that have been sliced off their main blocks on other pages. There are two adjustments that might solve the problem – changing the `Margins` and scaling the whole sheet up or down (done from `Setup...`) If neither of these work, you will have to do a major redesign!

Try these for a better fit

Back to the editing screen

'Next' may mean the page below the last, or the one at the top of the next strip

Zoom in to check details

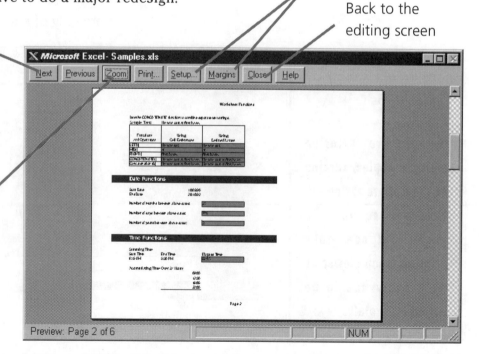

46

Word

When previewing a Word document, you may want to adjust font sizes, line spacing or the size and position of objects to get a better balanced page. You can do this. All the normal menu commands are available and extra toolbars can be added.

Tip

If you have an odd few lines on the last page, click Shrink to fit. This tries to fit the document onto one less page.

Multiple pages

Ruler (on/ off)

Shrink to fit

One page

Zoom level

Full screen (removes frame and menu bar)

Magnifier (toggles full page/close up)

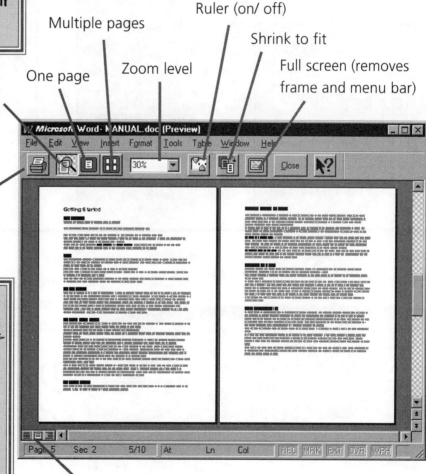

Print

Return to Normal or Page Layout View for easier editing

Take note

PowerPoint has no preview because each slide is designed as a single unit — its printed output will be the same as its screen appearance.

Page setup

It is always worth checking the Page setup before you print – especially if you are working from a Template, which may well have been designed for different paper or slide sizes to the ones you use.

Basic steps

1 Open the **File** menu and select **Page setup** or **Slide setup**

2 In Excel go to the **Paper** panel, in Word go to **Paper Size**

3 Select a **Paper size** from the list or specify a **Custom size**

4 Check the **Orientation** – *Portrait* or *Landscape*. In Powerpoint this may be different for **Slides** and **Notes**

5 For drafts, set the **Print quality** to the lowest dpi (dots per inch) value

① Select File– Page Setup

Take note

In Excel, you can adjust the scale of the printing so that the spreadsheet fits better on the paper.

Excel

② Open the Page panel

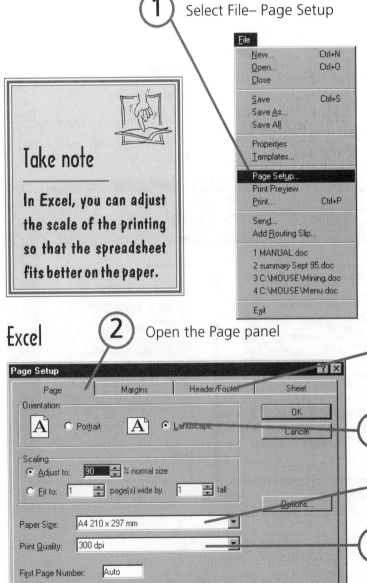

Headers and Footers are handled from within the document in Word

③ Upright or sideways?

④ Set the Paper size

⑤ Set low for drafts, high for final copies

48

Setting margins

In Excel or Word, you have a Margins panel where you can adjust the space around the printed area. Sometimes a slight reduction of margins will give you a better printout. There is little more irritating than a couple of odd lines of text or a tiny block of data on a separate sheet.

These largely duplicate options in the printer's Properties box

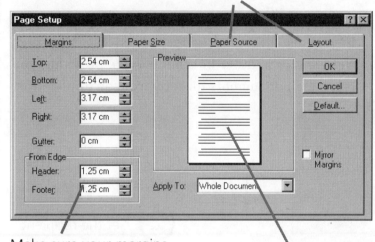

Make sure your margins don't overlap the Header/Footer spaces

The Preview gives a general idea of the printing area. To see how the actual document will look, use Print Preview.

(3) Upright or sideways?

(4) Set the Slide size

Files by wire

For 10 years or more, the experts have been telling us that computers will create the paperless office, but in most offices so far they seem to have created even more paper. If you are on a network, you could start to reverse that trend with Office 95. You can also help the move towards a paperless world!

- If you have a modem, you can send faxes directly from your PC.

- If you also have a connection to the Microsoft Network, or another Internet service provider, you can e-mail documents directly from an application.

Basic steps

- ❑ **E-mailing documents**
1 Open the **File** menu and select **Send**
2 Once Microsoft Exchange has loaded, click [To...]
3 Select the recipient from your **Address Book**
4 If you want to send copies, click [Cc...]
5 Type a brief header into the **Subject** line

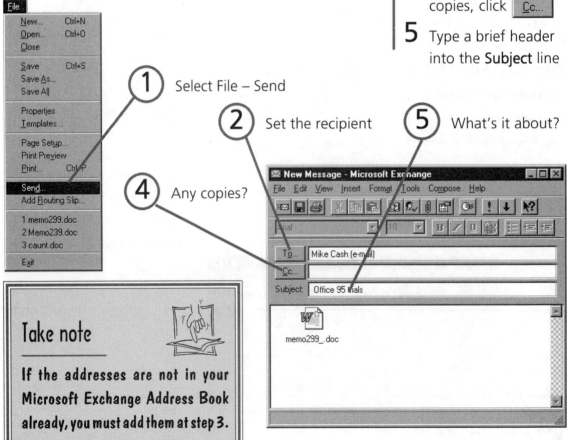

① Select File – Send

② Set the recipient

⑤ What's it about?

④ Any copies?

Take note

If the addresses are not in your Microsoft Exchange Address Book already, you must add them at step 3.

6 The e-mail will be stored in your Outbox

7 If you are already on-line, open the **Tools** menu, point to **Deliver Now Using** and select the connection.

Whether you send fax or e-mail depends upon how the address was set up

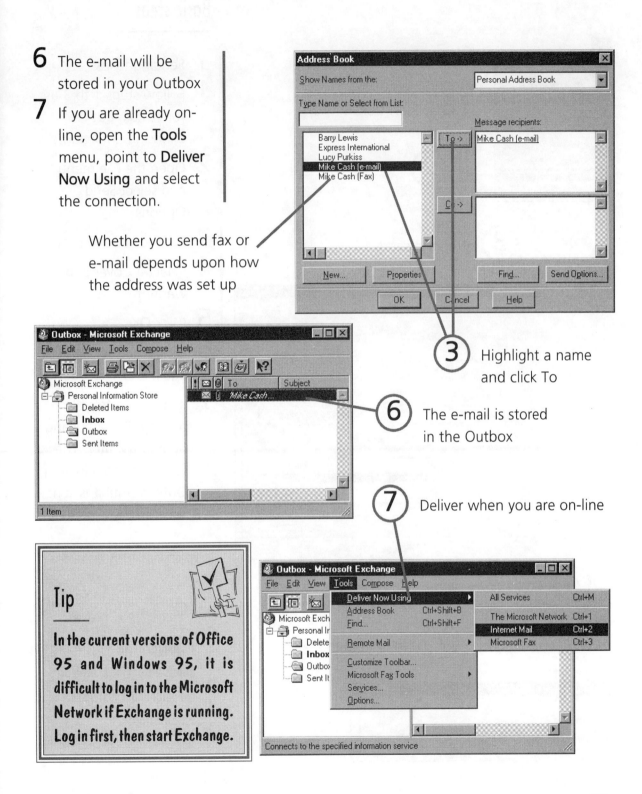

Address Book

Show Names from the: Personal Address Book

Type Name or Select from List:

Barry Lewis
Express International
Lucy Purkiss
Mike Cash (e-mail)
Mike Cash (Fax)

Message recipients:

To ->   Mike Cash (e-mail)

Cc ->

New...   Properties   Find...   Send Options...

OK   Cancel   Help

Outbox - Microsoft Exchange

File Edit View Tools Compose Help

Microsoft Exchange
Personal Information Store
Deleted Items
Inbox
Outbox
Sent Items

To   Subject

Mike Cash...

1 Item

③ Highlight a name and click To

⑥ The e-mail is stored in the Outbox

⑦ Deliver when you are on-line

Tip

In the current versions of Office 95 and Windows 95, it is difficult to log in to the Microsoft Network if Exchange is running. Log in first, then start Exchange.

Outbox - Microsoft Exchange

File Edit View Tools Compose Help

Deliver Now Using   All Services   Ctrl+M
Address Book   Ctrl+Shift+B   The Microsoft Network   Ctrl+1
Find...   Ctrl+Shift+F   Internet Mail   Ctrl+2
Remote Mail   Microsoft Fax   Ctrl+3
Customize Toolbar...
Microsoft Fax Tools
Services...
Options...

Microsoft Exch
Personal Ir
Delete
Inbox
Outbox
Sent It

Connects to the specified information service

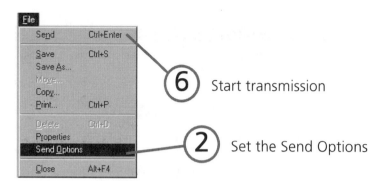

(6) Start transmission

(2) Set the Send Options

(3) When to send

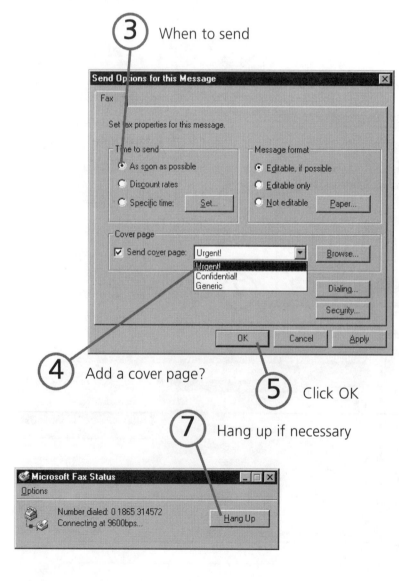

(4) Add a cover page?

(5) Click OK

(7) Hang up if necessary

Basic steps

- ❏ **Sending faxes**

1 Follow steps 1 to 3 as for e-mail, but choosing a fax address

2 Open the **File** menu and select **Send Options**

3 Set the Time to send

4 Select a **Cover page** if wanted.

5 Click **OK**

6 Open the **File** menu again and select **Send**

7 If you have trouble getting through **Hang up** and try later. The fax will remain in your Outbox until it is sent successfully.

Tip

For more on paperless communications, look out for Microsoft Networking Made Simple.

Basic steps

1 Open the **File** menu and select **Add Routing Slip**

2 Click [Address...] and select the first recipient from your Address Book

3 Repeat step 2 for any other recipients

4 Click [Route] to circulate the document immediately

or

5 Click [Add Slip] to leave it set for later routing

Routing slips

If you want several people to see and make comments on a draft document, you can circulate round the internal network, or through your Internet connections, by adding a Routing slip.

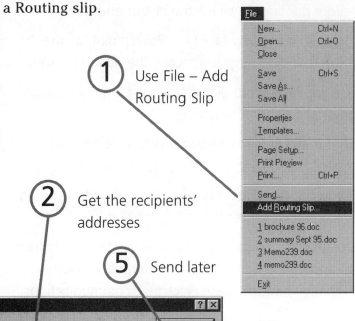

① Use File – Add Routing Slip

② Get the recipients' addresses

⑤ Send later

④ Send now

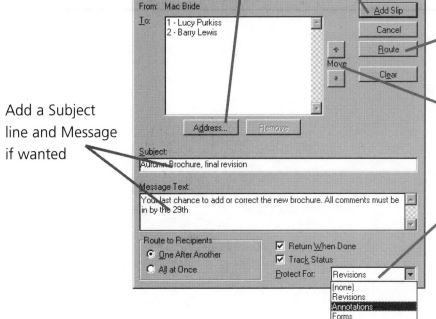

Add a Subject line and Message if wanted

Select the person and Move to adjust the routing order

Sets whether the readers can revise, annotate or not edit the document

Summary

❑ There are some differences in the printing routines, to suit the needs of the different applications.

❑ Always **Preview** your Excel and Word documents before printing, to check the layout and fit.

❑ There is no preview facility in **PowerPoint**, as the printed or slide output matches the screen display.

❑ Use the **Page setup** dialog box to set margins, paper orientation and print quality.

❑ Print **drafts** at lower resolutions to save time and toner.

❑ If you opt to **collate** multi-page documents, printing will be much slower.

❑ Documents can be sent by **e-mail** or **fax** directly from an application if you have a modem. Microsoft Exchange handles these electronic communications.

5 Working with text

Selecting text

There are essentially two approaches to formatting text.

- You can set the style, type the text, then turn it off, or set a new style.

- Or you can type in your text, then go back over it, selecting blocks and formatting them.

It is generally simplest to get the text typed first and format it to suit later – but before you can format it, you must select it.

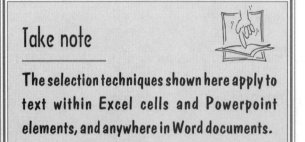

Take note

The selection techniques shown here apply to text within Excel cells and Powerpoint elements, and anywhere in Word documents.

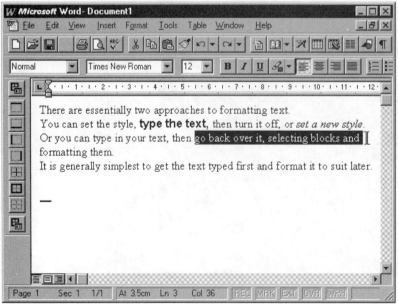

❏ **With a mouse**

1 Point to the start of the text to be selected

2 Hold the left mouse button down and drag to the last character

3 Release the mouse button

❏ **Click tricks**

1 Place the I-beam in a word

2 Double-click the left button to select the word

or

3 Triple-click to select the whole paragraph

❏ **With the [Shift] key**

1 Move the I-beam to the first character.

2 Hold down **[Shift]** and use the arrow keys to move the I-beam to the last character

3 Release **[Shift]**

Select whole columns by
selecting their letters

Click here to select
the whole sheet

Select whole rows
by selecting their
numbers

You can select and
format a block
within a cell

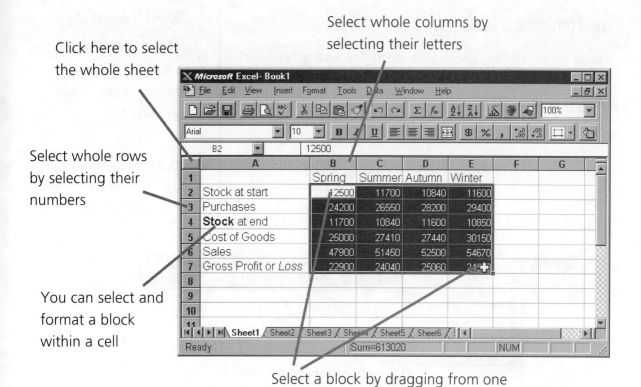

Select a block by dragging from one
corner to the opposite

To select one or more
elements, drag an outline
to enclose them

Blocks within the text
can be selected in the
usual ways

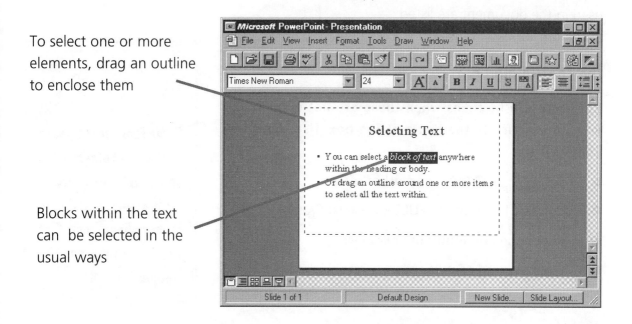

Fonts

The Formatting Toolbars

These hold all the tools you need for everyday work. There are minor differences between the applications, reflecting their different requirements.

Styles
(*page 63*)

Font name   Bold   Underline

Size in points   Italics   Highlight
(Word only)

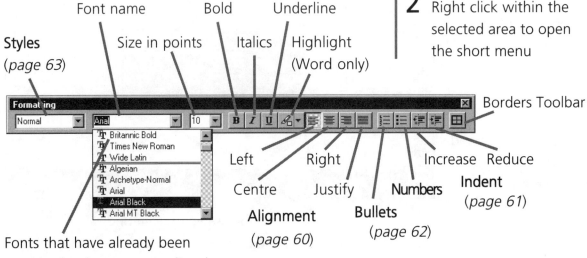

Borders Toolbar

Left   Right   Increase Reduce

Centre   Justify   **Numbers** **Indent**
(*page 61*)

Alignment   **Bullets**
(*page 60*)   (*page 62*)

Fonts that have already been used in the document are listed at the top for easy re-use.

The Fonts dialog box

But there will be times when these are not enough and you should turn to the Fonts dialog box. Use this when you want to:

- set $_{subscript,}$ ^{superscript}, and other effects
- convert headings to FULL or SMALL CAPITALS
- check the suitability of a **new font**
- use coloured text

Basic steps

1 Select the text to be formatted

2 Click the Toolbar buttons to set fonts and styles

or

2 Right click within the selected area to open the short menu

Tip

Some fonts are larger or heavier than others of the same size and style. That's why you should always choose your font before changing the settings.

3 Select **Font** (**Format cells** in Excel)

4 Switch to the **Font** panel if it is not already open

5 If you are going to change the font, *do this first*

6 Set other effects as required, checking the appearance in the Preview pane

7 Click **OK**

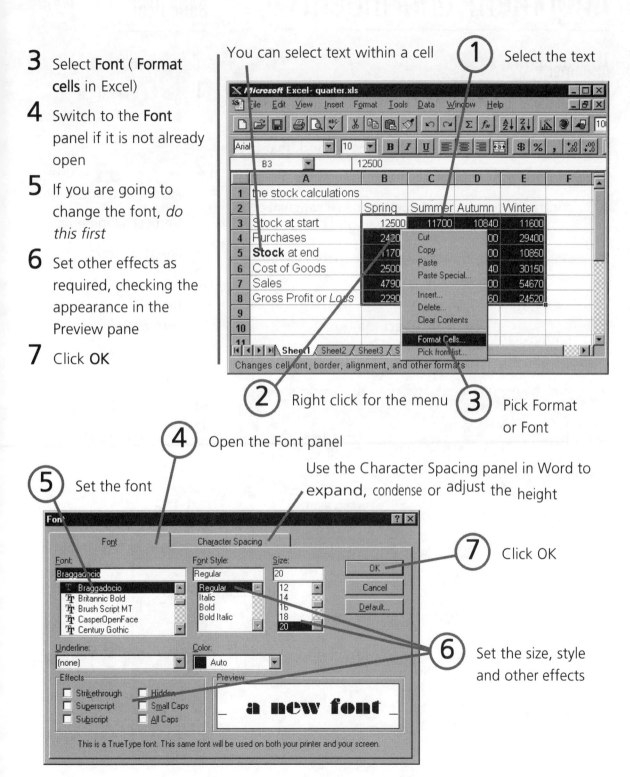

You can select text within a cell

① Select the text

② Right click for the menu

③ Pick Format or Font

④ Open the Font panel

⑤ Set the font

Use the Character Spacing panel in Word to expand, condense or adjust the height

⑦ Click OK

⑥ Set the size, style and other effects

Alignment and Indents

Alignment

This refers to how text fits against the margins (or the edges of Excel cells). Four options are always available: Left, Right, Centre and Justify (aligned to both margins)

Excel also has other options to handle headings. You can:

● centre the text from one cell across a range of cells, perhaps to give a table a heading;

● set column labels vertical, aligned to the top, bottom or centrally in the row.

❑ **Centred headings**

1 Select the range of cells that the text is to be centred in

2 Click the 🔳 **Centre Across Columns** button

❑ **Vertical alignments**

1 Select the text

2 Right click for the menu and select **Format Cells..**

3 Open the **Alignment** panel

4 Set the **Orientation**

5 Set the **Vertical** alignment

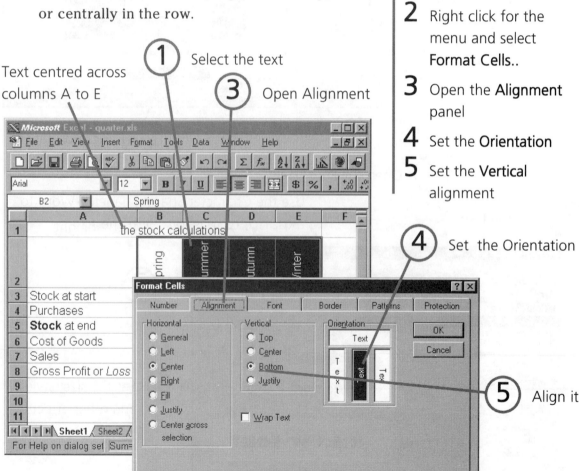

Text centred across columns A to E

① Select the text

③ Open Alignment

④ Set the Orientation

⑤ Align it

60

Basic steps

Indents

1 Select the text

2 Click ![Word indent icon] (Word) or
![PowerPoint indent icon] (PowerPoint) to
indent

or

3 Click ![Word outdent icon] (Word) or
![PowerPoint outdent icon] (Powerpoint) to
pull back out

Indents do not apply in Excel, where it is cells, not margins, that frame the text. They do apply in Word and PowerPoint, and they do not merely set the distance from the edge, they also create a structure.

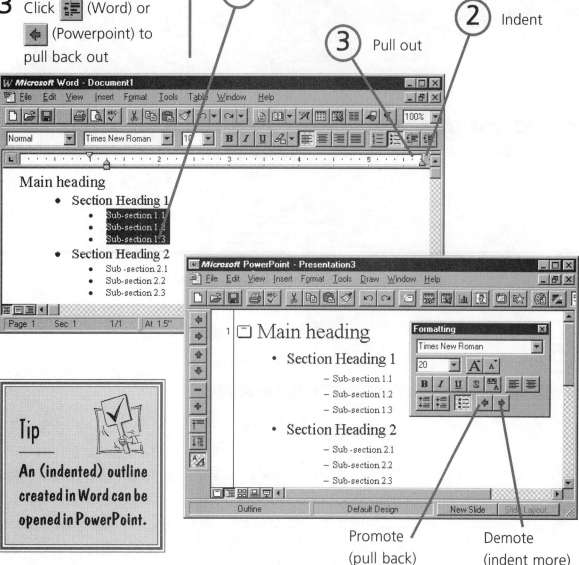

① Select the text

② Indent

③ Pull out

Promote
(pull back)

Demote
(indent more)

Tip

An (indented) outline
created in Word can be
opened in PowerPoint.

Bullets

In Word, a list can have bullets added by clicking ▤ or through Format – Bullets and Numbering. Use the second method if you want to pick your own bullets

③ Set the basic style   ④ Click Modify

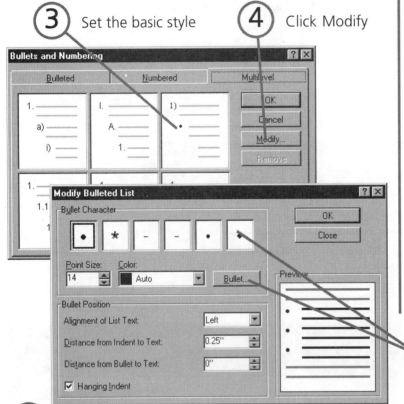

⑥ Set the font   ⑦ Double-click to select

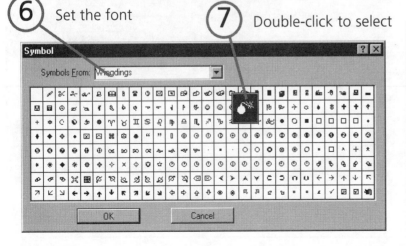

1 Select the text

2 Open the **Format** menu and select **Bullets and Numbering**

3 Select the basic style from one of the panels

4 Click [Modify...]

5 Pick one from the set, or click [Bullet...] for more

6 Select a font – try Symbol or Wingdings

7 Hold the mouse button down for a close up of the bullets – double-click to select one

⑤ Pick a bullet

Tip

To change bullets in PowerPoint, use Format – Bullets. It takes you to a font display much like that in Word

Basic steps

☐ **Excel – applying a style**

1 Select the text or cells

2 Open the **Format** menu and select **Styles**

3 At the **Styles** dialog box, pick one from the **Style Name** list

4 Click **OK**

☐ **Creating a new style**

5 Type in a **Style Name**

6 Select the aspect to be changed and click
[Modify...]

7 Edit the settings

8 If you want to change another aspect, open its panel

9 Click **OK** then

A *style* is a combination of font, size, alignment and indent options. Word and Excel both come with a range of pre-defined styles, and you can modify these or add your own to the sets. Applying a style is a matter of a couple of clicks; creating a new style is almost as simple.

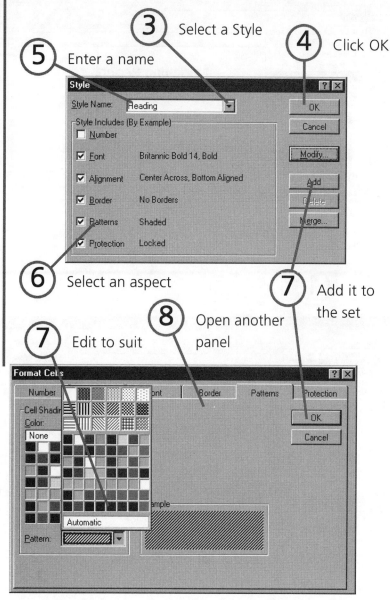

③ Select a Style

④ Click OK

⑤ Enter a name

⑥ Select an aspect

⑦ Add it to the set

⑦ Edit to suit

⑧ Open another panel

Tip

To modify a style, select it from the list then follow the New styles steps 6-9.

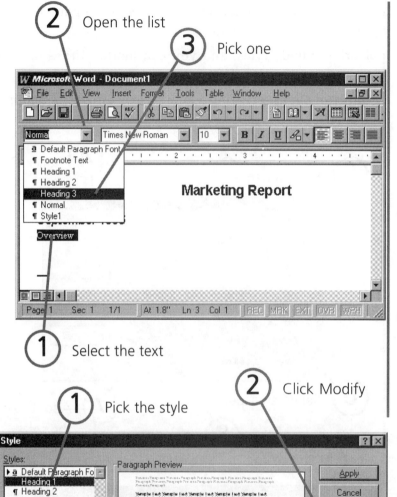

② Open the list

③ Pick one

Marketing Report

① Select the text

□ **Word – applying a style**

1 Select the text

either

2 Drop down the **Styles**

3 Pick one from the list

or, if the style is not in the drop-down list

4 Open the **Format** menu and select **Styles**

5 At the Style dialog box, pick one from the list

□ **Word – modifying a style**

1 At the **Style** dialog box, pick the style from the list

2 Click [Modify...]

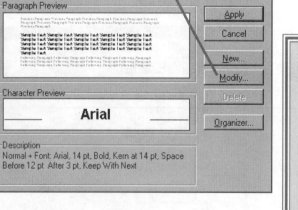

① Pick the style

② Click Modify

Switch to the full list of **All Styles**
if you can't see the one you want.

Take note

A style applies to the whole paragraph, and you can select one paragraph by putting the I-beam anywhere within it.

3 Click [Format ▼] to open the menu and select the aspect to be changed

4 Edit the settings

5 Repeat 3 and 4 as necessary

6 Click **OK**, and [Apply] at the **Style** dialog box

❑ **Creating a style**

7 At the **Style** dialog box, click [New...]

8 Type in a Name

9 Continue as for modifying, from step 3

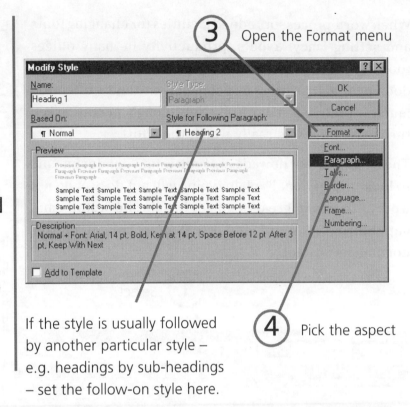

③ Open the Format menu

④ Pick the aspect

If the style is usually followed by another particular style – e.g. headings by sub-headings – set the follow-on style here.

PowerPoint

PowerPoint does not use named styles, but it does allow you to pick up the style of one text item and apply it to another.

Copy the current text style

Apply it to another item

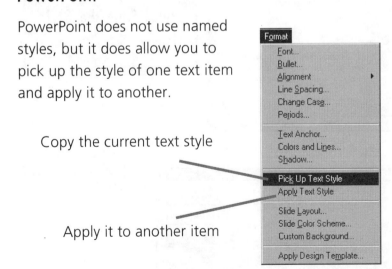

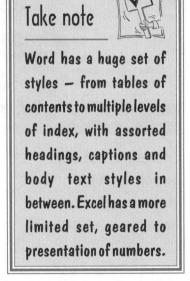

Autoformats

When word-processors added facilities for changing fonts and setting fancy layouts, productivity in many offices took a great leap *backwards*. Instead of simply typing the document and printing it, people spent time – often too much – prettying it up first. Not enough people asked themselves if it was really worth the effort.

The trouble is that nowadays, if you want your documents to look "professional", plain typing will not do. But do not worry, here's a great leap forward. The autoformat capabilities of Word and Excel give you attractive documents *instantly*.

Basic steps

❑ **Word Autoformat**

1 Open the **Format** menu and select **Autoformat**

2 Click **OK** to run the basic formatting.

Take note

Autoformat works in two stages. First it applies styles – Heading, Normal, Caption, etc – to the different blocks of text. Then you pick a suite of styles from the Style Gallery.

① Select

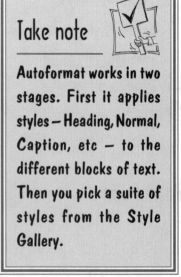

Autoformat **Options** control the automatic replacement of special characters – see page 72

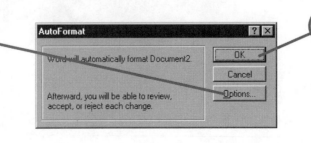

② Click OK

Basic steps

3 When you get the **Formatting completed** message, click

    Style Gallery...

4 At the **Style Gallery**, select a style, checking it in the preview screen

5 Click **OK** when you find one you like

6 Click Accept

③ Open the Style Gallery

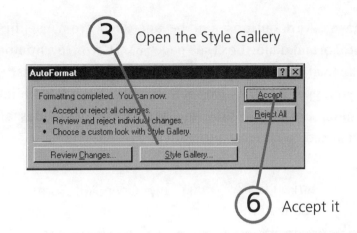

⑥ Accept it

④ Check out the Styles

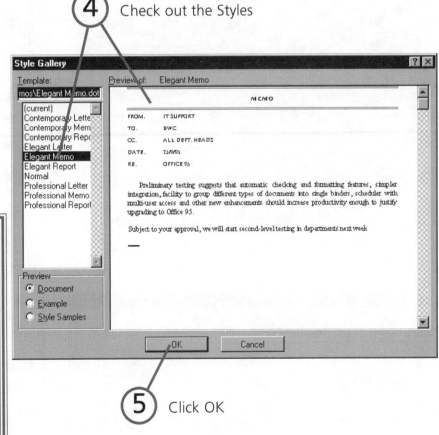

⑤ Click OK

AutoFormat As You Type

These Word options can be accessed from the first AutoFormat dialog box (see page 66). There are a number of special characters and symbols which can be replaced as you type. You can also set it to create lists. Add bullets or numbers to the first line and subsequent lines are formatted to match, automatically.

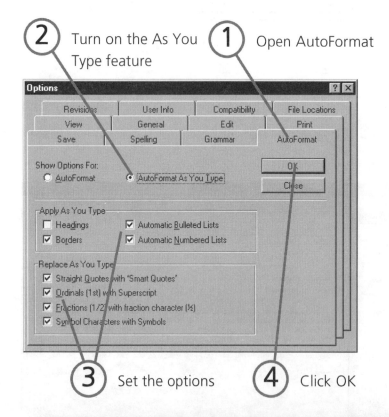

② Turn on the As You Type feature

① Open AutoFormat

③ Set the options

④ Click OK

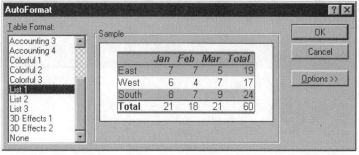

(see page 66)

Basic steps

1 Open the **Autoformat** options panel

2 Turn on **Autoformat As You Type**

3 Set the **Apply** and **Replace As You Type** options as required.

4 Click **OK**

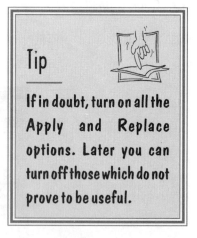

Tip

If in doubt, turn on all the **Apply** and **Replace** options. Later you can turn off those which do not prove to be useful.

Excel AutoFormat

Excel has a wide range of ready made formats for tables of data. Select the table, give the Format – AutoFormat command and select a style from the list.

68

Undo

In the old days, you were lucky if your software allowed you to undo a mistake. With the Office applications you can go back and undo a whole string of actions. This doesn't just protect you from the results of hasty decisions or self-willed mice, it gives you a freedom to experiment. You can do major editing or reformatting, and if at the end you preferred things how they were, you can undo your way back to it.

Redo

This is the undo-undo button! If you undid to much, use this to put it back again.

Open the list, then select
the actions to undo

Redo last undone action

Undo the last action

Select from the Redo list

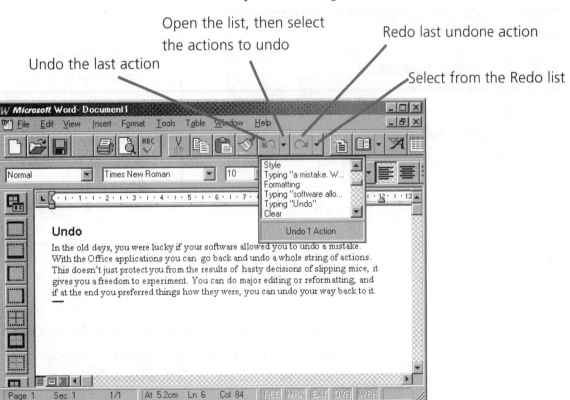

Spellcheck

The main spell checking system is available in all Office applications. There is a good dictionary behind it, but it does not cover everything. Proper names, technical terms and esoteric words may well be unrecognised and be thrown up as 'errors'.

Word has an additional check-as-you-type facility (see opposite). Even in Word, it is often best to run a spell check after you have finished typing – especially if you have a lot of typing to do and need to watch the keyboard rather than the screen!

1 If you want to check **part** of a document, or a block of cells in a spreadsheet, select it

2 Open the **Tools** menu and select **Spelling** or click [ABC✓]

❑ When a word is not recognised you can:

3 Select a suggestion and click [Change]

or

4 If it is a valid word click [Ignore]

or

5 [Add] to put it in a custom dictionary

or

6 Click in the **Not in Dictionary** slot to copy the word into the **Change To** slot, edit it then click [Change]

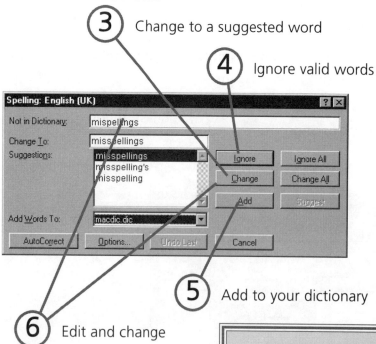

③ Change to a suggested word

④ Ignore valid words

⑤ Add to your dictionary

⑥ Edit and change

Take note

If you haven't already set up a dictionary for your own special words, click the Options button to open the Spelling options panel and use the Custom Dictionaries button.

Basic steps

Word's automatic spell checking

1 Open the **Tools** menu and select **Options**

2 Switch to the **Spelling** panel

3 Turn on **Automatic Spell Checking**

❑ **While you type**

4 Right click on an underlined word

5 If the menu has a suitable suggestion, click on it to correct your mistake.

6 If there are no suggestions, click on **Spellings** to open the Spelling dialog box.

If you turn this option on, misspellings are spotted as you type and can be corrected immediately.

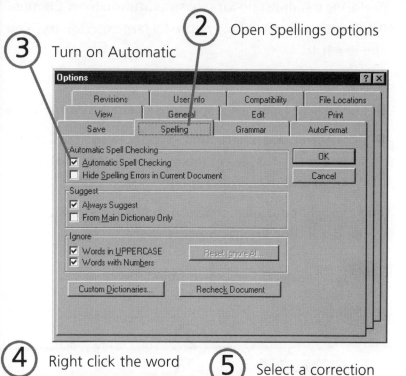

71

AutoCorrect

Don't confuse this with the spell checker. There are similarities, in that both correct typing, but AutoCorrect performs a simple one-for-one substitution from a limited list, rather than checking against a large dictionary. You can use it to:

- correct common transpositions – **teh** into **the**

- correct common misspellings – **acheive** into **achieve**

- call up special characters – type **(c)** and AutoCorrect swaps it for **©**. (These are also handled by AutoFormat As You Type.)

You can add your own common 'typos' or substitutions to the list if they are not already there.

Basic steps

1 Pull down the **Tools** menu and select **AutoCorrect...**

2 Put a tick by **Replace Text as You Type**

❑ **Adding to the list**

3 Enter the error or a character combination into the **Replace** slot

4 Type the substition in the **With** slot

5 Click [Add]

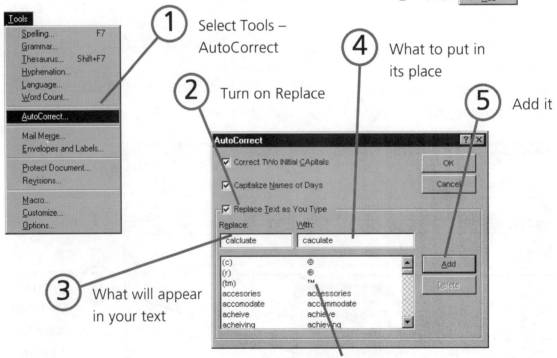

① Select Tools – AutoCorrect

② Turn on Replace

③ What will appear in your text

④ What to put in its place

⑤ Add it

You can get special characters from Windows' Character Map, if you want to add more

Exceptions for Capitalising

Word's version of AutoCorrect also checks that the first letter of sentences are capitals. As a sentence is defined as something that comes after a full stop, abbreviations can create problems. The solution is to have a list of abbreviations and not capitalise words that follow them. You can add to this list.

Are the other Capital rules right for you?

① Click Exceptions

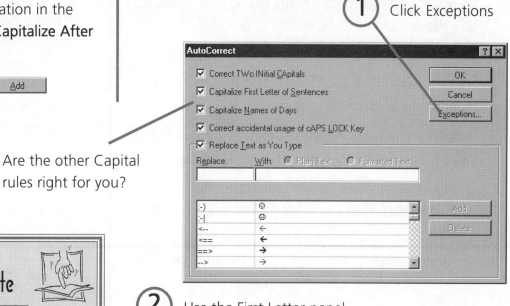

② Use the First Letter panel

③ Type the abbreviation

④ Add it

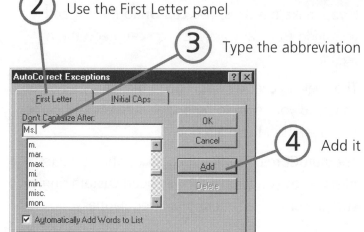

Summary

- **Text** can be selected with either the mouse or keys, or a combination of both. **Objects** can be selected by clicking on them, or dragging an outline round them with the mouse. The **same selection techniques** apply in all applications.

- **Font** types, sizes and styles can be set from the Formatting toolbar or the Fonts dialog box. The dialog box also has additional control options.

- Text can be **aligned** to the Left or Right margins, Centred between them or Justified up to both.

- **Indents** give a structure to text.

- **Bullets** can be easily added to lists. The default bullets can be replaced by any characters you choose.

- Excel and Word have ready made **styles** that can be applied to text. They can be modified and new ones created.

- The **Autoformat** facility gives you standard formats for common documents and tables of data.

- If you make mistakes, you can **Undo** them – and if you undo too many actions, you can **Redo** them again.

- The **Spelling checker** has a good dictionary, and you can build your own to hold special terms and names that are not in the main one.

- The **AutoCorrect** routine recognises and corrects mistakes as you type. This may need customising to stop it 'correcting' intentional irregularities.

6 Sharing data

Alternative approaches

There are a number of different ways to share data between applications. The first three bring a selected object or block of data into a second application. They use the Edit Copy and Paste commands in various ways.

- **Simple copying** – the pasted-in text, table, picture or whatever becomes an integral part of the host document, dropping all connection to the application in which it was created. Use this method where the only editing or reformatting that you might want to do to the pasted-in data can be done from within the new application – documents to be printed, e-mailed or copied for circulation.

- **Embedding** – the pasted-in data forms an independent object within the document. It loses its connection to the original data, but can be edited by its creating application *within the host document*. Use this method if you want to be able to edit the object using its original application.

- **Linking** – the pasted-in data retains a full connection to the original data and its application. Any changes in the source data are automatically reflected in the copy, and the original file can be edited – by calling up its application – from within the host document. This is the method to use for reports and presentations where you want to ensure that all the data is up to date.

Take note

Most of the methods described here use OLE – Object Linking and Embedding. This is a standard Windows facility that can be used for sharing data between any Windows applications, not just the Office 95 set.

Copy and Paste

The first step in sharing data is to go to the source document, select the object or block of text and copy it, using either the **Edit – Copy** command or 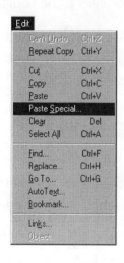. What you do then depends upon whether you want to copy, embed or link the data, and what format you want it in.

- Use 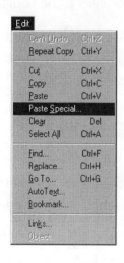 or **Edit – Paste** to copy in the data, using the default format. This will be either Formatted Text or Picture, as applicable.

- Use **Edit – Paste Special** to embed or link, or to select your own format for copied data.

Paste As formats

Word, Excel, PowerPoint (or other) **Object** – use this for embedding

Formatted Text – the text retains its fonts, styles, etc, but may be edited by the host application.

Unformatted Text – plain text, editable by the host.

Picture and **Bitmap** – scalable graphics; Pictures can give better printed images.

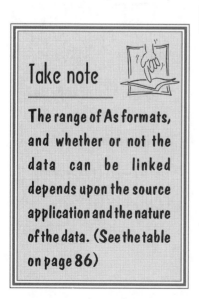

Take note

The range of As formats, and whether or not the data can be linked depends upon the source application and the nature of the data. (See the table on page 86)

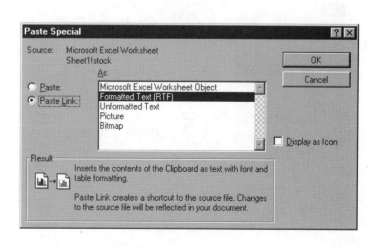

Copying

Using the  and ▦ buttons is the quickest and simplest way to get data from one application into another, but the data is pasted differently in different applications.

1 In the source application, select the object or block of text or cells to be copied

2 Click ▦ or pull down the **Edit** menu and select **Copy**

3 Go to the host document

4 To paste as *text*, point the cursor to where the data is to be placed

5 click ▦ or pull down the **Edit** menu and select **Paste**

① Select the data

② Copy it

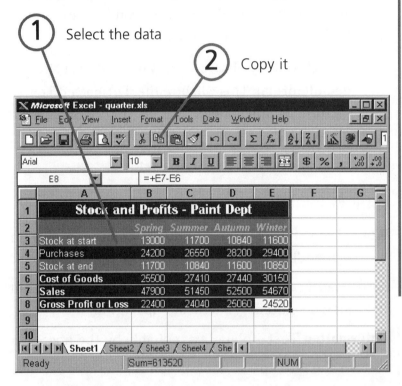

② Copy to the Clipboard

⑤ Paste into place

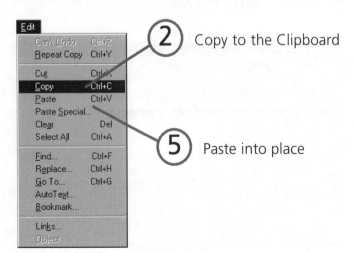

Tip

If you do a lot of copy and paste work, learn the keyboard shortcuts:

[Ctrl] – [C] to Copy

[Ctrl] – [V] to Paste

Excel to Word

Tip

If you want to import the data as a picture, use **Paste Special.**

brings in the data in Rich Text Format, and creates a Word table.

● As it is text, it can be edited within Word in the usual fashion.

● As it is Rich Text, its font, size, borders, etc are retained.

④ Position the cursor

⑤ Paste in the data

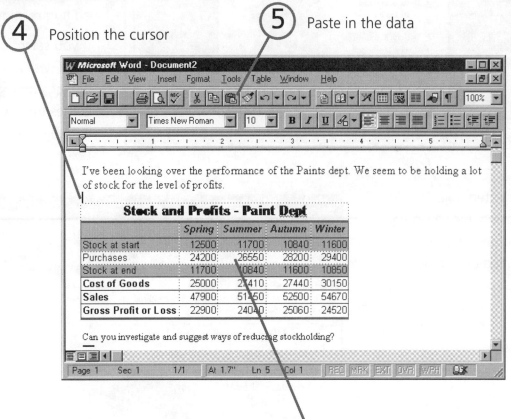

Individual columns and rows, and the contents of any of the cells can be edited and reformatted as needed.

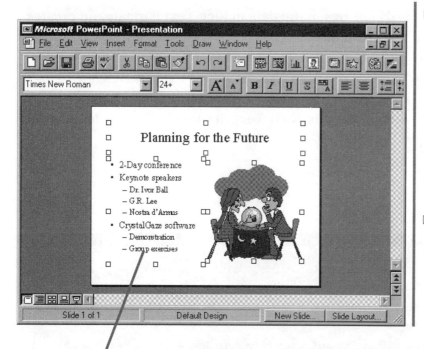

□ If you select one or more objects from a slide, then 📋 into Word, the objects come in as a single picture. You can edit this to some extent, using Word's picture editing routines.

□ If you select the text, from within a text object, then 📋, it comes into Word as editable, formatted text.

Selected objects are pasted in as a single picture. This can be scaled or cropped to size.

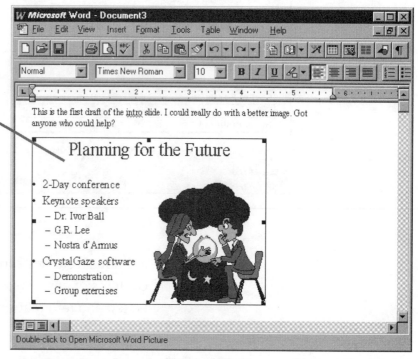

Word to PowerPoint

- ❑ If you 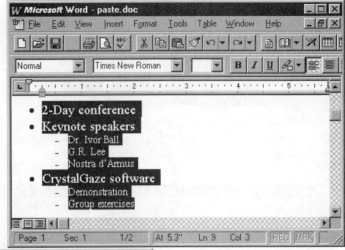 Word text into a text object, it is copied in text, losing much of its original formatting.

- ❑ If you draw an outline and 📋, the data comes in as an *embedded* Word object. (See page 82)

This text can be edited directly in PowerPoint

Outline drawn first

To edit this, double-click to call up Word.

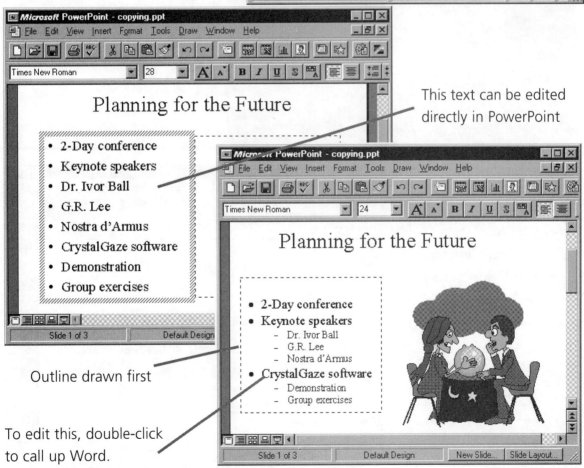

Embedding

On the previous pages, we noticed that embedding occurs when you paste Word text *as an object* into a presentation, but not when you paste PowerPoint objects into Word. To be certain that an object is embedded, it is best use the Paste Special command.

Basic steps

1 Select the object to be pasted

2 Back in the host document, open the Edit menu and select **Paste Special..**

3 Set the **As** option to an **Object** of the original application

4 Select **Paste**

5 Click **OK**

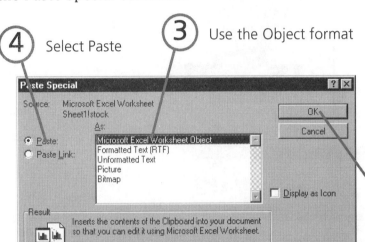

④ Select Paste

③ Use the Object format

⑤ Click OK

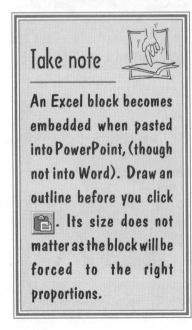

Take note

An Excel block becomes embedded when pasted into PowerPoint, (though not into Word). Draw an outline before you click 📋. Its size does not matter as the block will be forced to the right proportions.

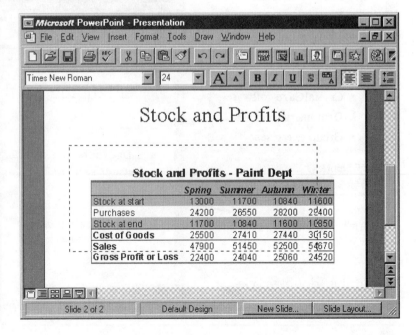

Editing embedded objects

1 Double click on the
embedded object to
open a (limited) version
of its application

or

2 Right click to open the
short menu and choose
Edit ...

3 Right click again for a
short menu of editing
commands, if wanted

4 Click anywhere on the
document to close the
embedded application.

Working with the tools of the host document's application,
the only changes you can make to an embedded object
are its size and position. If you want to edit or reformat its
content, you must call up its original application.

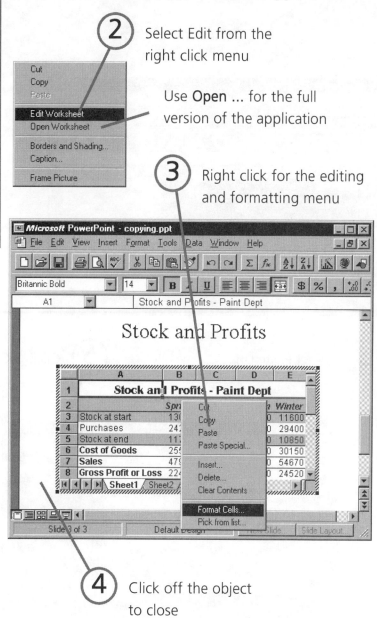

② Select Edit from the
right click menu

Use **Open** ... for the full
version of the application

③ Right click for the editing
and formatting menu

Take note

**The embedded object is
only a copy of the original
data. If you edit an
embedded object, it does
not affect the data in the
original file and vice
versa.**

④ Click off the object
to close

Linking

The one crucial difference between embedding and linking is that with a linked object, there is only one set of data. When you edit the original file – the source data – the contents of the linked object are changed to match.

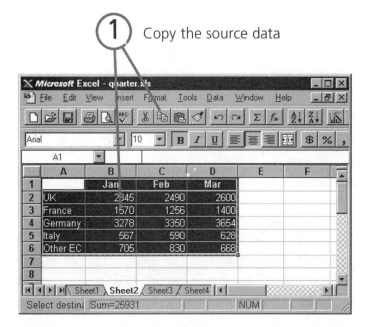

1 Copy the source data

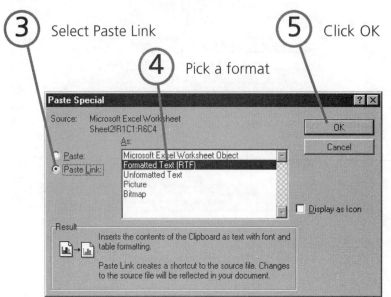

3 Select Paste Link

4 Pick a format

5 Click OK

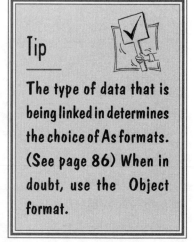

Tip

The type of data that is being linked in determines the choice of As formats. (See page 86) When in doubt, use the Object format.

Editing linked objects

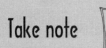
All linked objects can be edited by double-clicking on them to call up their original application. Those pasted in the Object format can only be edited this way.

In Object, Picture or Bitmap format, you can alter the size and position of the linked boject.

With Formatted or Plain Text, you can also edit them using the host application's tools – though these edits will only last until the link is updated. This is only worth doing if you want to prettify something for immediate printing.

The month names have been edited to appear in ~~~~~~~~~~ ect. ~~~~~~~ the ~~~~~~ .) ~~~~~~ s that ~~~~~~ or when ~~~~~~ned, the link ~~~~~~ed and the original headings restored.

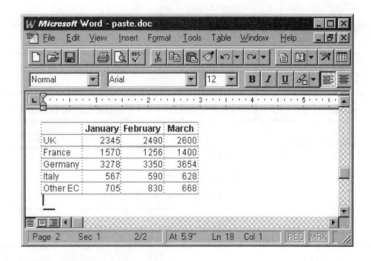

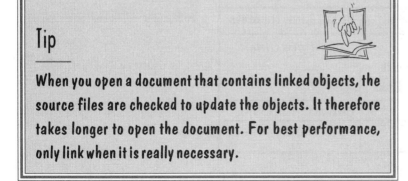

Tip

When you open a document that contains linked objects, the source files are checked to update the objects. It therefore takes longer to open the document. For best performance, only link when it is really necessary.

Paste/Paste Link formats

The As formats for Pasting vary with the nature of the data and the source application. They are generally – but not always – what you might expect.

Word

Data type	Paste formats	Paste Link formats
Text	Picture Formatted Text Unformatted Text	Word Object
Table	Picture Formatted Text Unformatted Text	Word Object
Drawing	Picture	*not possible*

Excel

Data type	Paste formats	Paste Link formats
Cell block	Picture Bitmap Formatted Text Unformatted Text	Excel Object *see note*
Graph	Picture	Excel Object

PowerPoint

Data type	Paste formats	Paste Link formats
Text	Picture Formatted Text Unformatted Text	*not possible*
Slide	Picture	PowerPoint Object
Element	Picture	PowerPoint Object

Take note

When embedding, you can only ever use the Object format.

Take note

A block of cells from Excel can be linked into Word in any of the Paste formats, but only as an Object into PowerPoint.

Inserted objects

Complete files can be linked into documents using the **Insert Object** command. Though the whole file is linked, not all of it will be displayed – you will see part of a Word or Excel document, or the first slide of a presentation. If you edit it, you can access the rest, or scroll to a different part of the document to change the visible area.

Inserted file objects can be:

● created at the time, from within the host document, or loaded in from file.

● either embedded or linked.

● displayed normally or shown as icons. In either case, the Edit and Open options for the source application are on the short menu.

Word

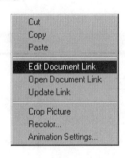

The selected options are what you get if you simply double-click on an inserted option.

PowerPoint

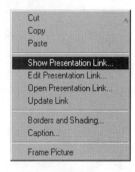

Excel

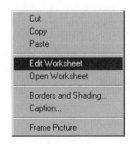

Edit and Open both call up the full application in Excel and PowerPoint.

Inserting an object

Once you have decided what you want to insert, and whether to place it as an icon or displayed object, the actual insertion is easy.

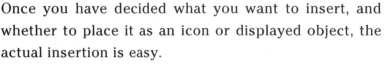

Use Insert – Object

Open the Create from File panel

Browse for the file

1 Open the **Insert** menu and select **Object**

2 Switch to the **Create from File** panel (it's an option in PowerPoint)

3 Click [Browse...] to locate the file

4 Turn on **Link to file**, if wanted, or leave it off to embed the file

5 If you want the file as a visible object, click **OK**

Link or embed?

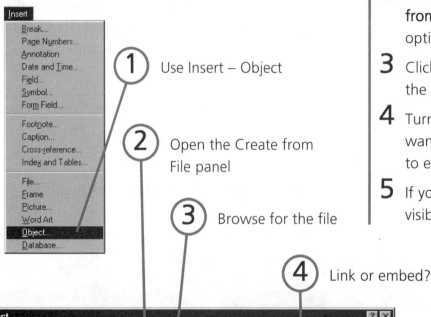

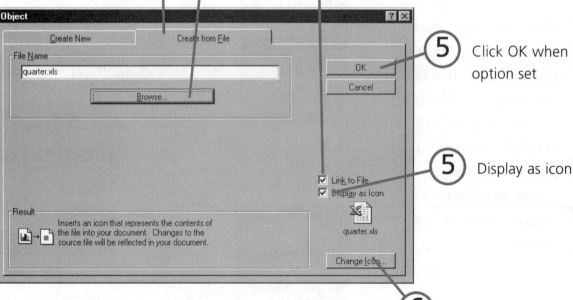

Click OK when option set

Display as icon

Click to edit icon

88

Basic steps

Icons for links

1 Follow steps 1-4 opposite

5 Turn on the **Display as Icon** option

6 Click [Change Icon...]

7 Check out icons in the list to see if there is one you prefer

8 Replace the filename with a brief **Caption**

9 Click **OK**

If you want your readers to open (or run) the linked file to see it properly, it may be better to place it as an icon. Most computer users nowadays need little prompting to click an icon, though they may well need prompting to click on a spreadsheet table, block of text or other image.

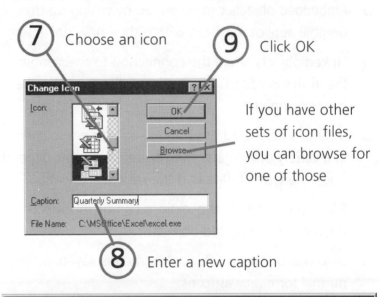

⑦ Choose an icon

⑨ Click OK

If you have other sets of icon files, you can browse for one of those

⑧ Enter a new caption

Tip

Few people can resist clicking icons to find out what's there. Prompting is rarely necessary.

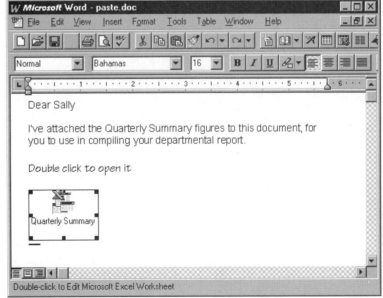

89

Summary

❑ The **Edit – Copy** and **Paste** commands can be used to copy data from one application to another. Depending upon the type of data and the applications, the copy may become an integral part of the target document, or may be embedded in it.

❑ **Embedded** objects can be edited by calling up their original application from within their new document.

❑ **Linked** objects retain the connection to their original file. If this is edited, the changes will be seen in the new document.

❑ Data can be pasted or paste linked into a document, in a **variety of formats**. The choice of formats depends upon the type of data and the source application.

❑ Files from different applications can be included in documents as **Inserted objects**.

❑ Linked and Inserted objects can be displayed in their normal format or as **icons.**

7 Binders

Binders and sections

The concept of the Binder is simple but effective. If you have a number of documents – from the same or different Office applications – that are regularly used together, you can store them in one binder file, rather than in separate application files.

Working in the Binder, you can:

- keep related files together, opening and saving all the documents in one operation;

- print all of the documents at once – though selected documents can also be printed individually;

- switch quickly and easily from one application to another;

- copy formats, styles and data between documents more easily.

Sections

The documents in a binder file are referred to as *sections*. Once it has been set up, you would normally leave the composition of a binder alone, but it is not fixed permanently. An existing file can be inserted into a binder as a new section, and sections, created within a binder, can be saved as separate files.

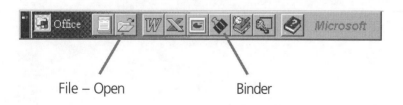

File – Open   Binder

Tip

As with any Office application, you can open a binder document from the File – Open shortcut tool, but it is often easier to work from the Binder shortcut.

92

The Binder display

The Binder itself is little more than a means of holding and accessing documents. It offers an almost blank display and a limited menu. Once you have opened a binder file, the display will be dominated by the application of the current document within the binder.

The slim panel down the left side is the means of switching between documents. It can be tucked out of the way when not needed, by clicking ⬌ on the far left of the menu bar.

The Section menu has options for adding documents to a new binder

The Section menu is added to every application's menu bar

Click to close and reopen the control panel

Click to switch to the document

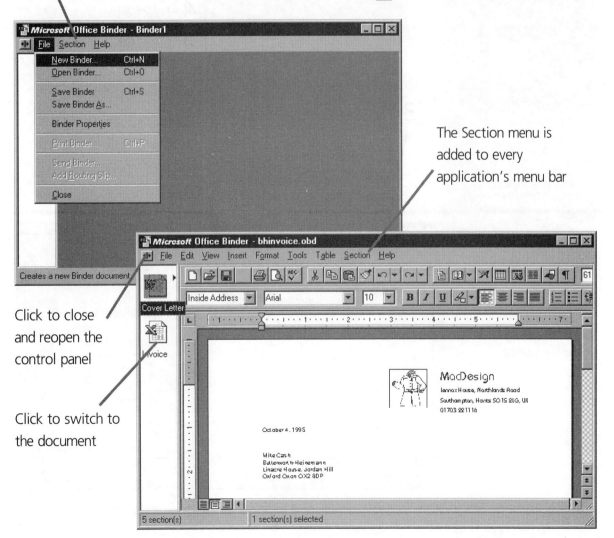

Ready made binders

Office 95 comes with a small set of ready-made binders that – even if they don't exactly meet your needs – can be adapted to suit. If you do not intend to use them, still have a look at them, as they serve to demonstrate some of the key concepts.

Basic steps

1 Click  on the Shortcut bar to start the Binder

2 Open the **File** menu and select **New**

3 Switch to the **Binders** panel

4 Select a file

5 Click **OK**

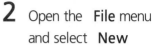

② Use File – New

③ Open the Binders panel

④ Select a file

The Preview shows the layout and style of the first document in the binder

An OBZ file is a wizard; OBT files are Templates

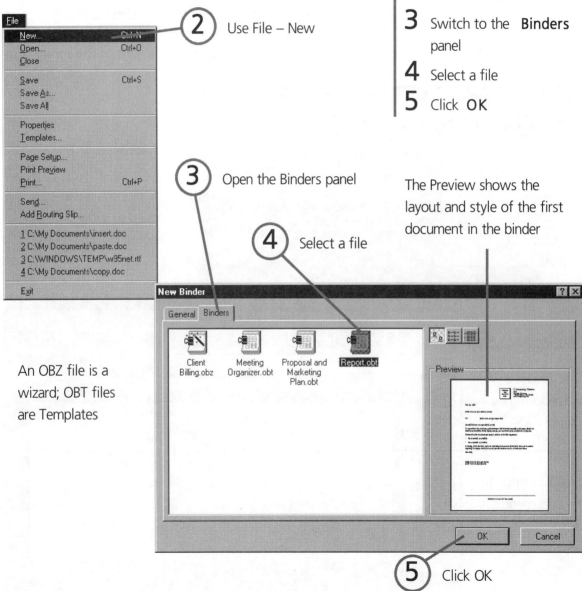

⑤ Click OK

Client Billing

This is a wizard which can generate a Fax Cover, Cover Letter (Word), Invoice, Timecard and Materials card (Excel). It collects details of your company and your client. (The data is retained, so that if you run the wizard again – for another client's bill – you will not have to reenter your company details.) At the final stage it customises each of the documents, using a standard – and good-looking – format.

Take note

Excel templates are geared to US business needs and may need minor alterations for UK use. In this invoice you will have to remove references to State and Local taxes, replacing one with VAT.

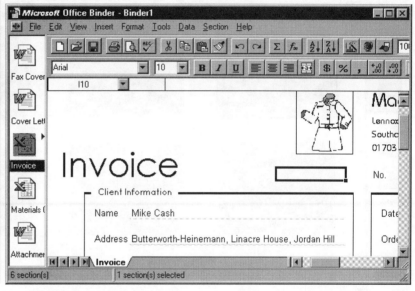

Meeting Organizer

This binder has templates for an Invitation, Agenda, Minutes and Memo (Word), a PowerPoint Slide Show, and an Excel-based address list.

The styles are formal and business-like, but even if you do not like the layouts and formats, these are worth seeing for the sound advice and guidelines that are incorporated in their sample texts.

Report

This is one of the least specific templates – inevitably so, as a report could be about almost anything to almost any audience. There are three Word documents – Cover Letter, Executive Summary and Analysis – an Excel 'Data' sheet and a Slide Show.

With the Slide Show template, you don't just get layout and formatting, you also get a sensible outline to work to.

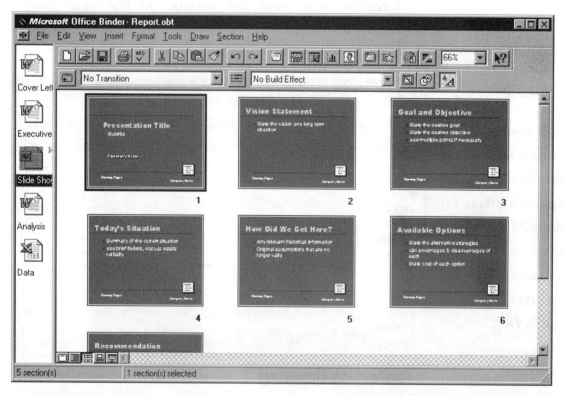

Proposal and Marketing Plan

This binder contains a Cover Letter, Referrals, Details and Follow up (Word), plus an Excel Quote and a Slide Show. As with the others, the guidance written in the documents may be worth as much as the formatting.

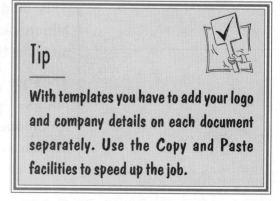

Tip

With templates you have to add your logo and company details on each document separately. Use the Copy and Paste facilities to speed up the job.

Creating a new binder

1 Click ⬡ on the
Shortcut bar

or if you already have a
binder open

2 Click 🗋 on an
application's toolbar

❏ **To create a document**

3 Pull down the **Section**
menu and select **Add**

4 Select the application
type from the **Add**
Section panel

❏ **To use an existing**
document

5 Pull down the **Section**
menu and select **Add**
from File

6 At the Add from File
dialog box, pick a file

7 Click   Add

If none of the templates meet your needs, you can create
a new binder from scratch. The documents that are
bound into it can also be created from scratch – within
the binder – or pulled in from existing files.

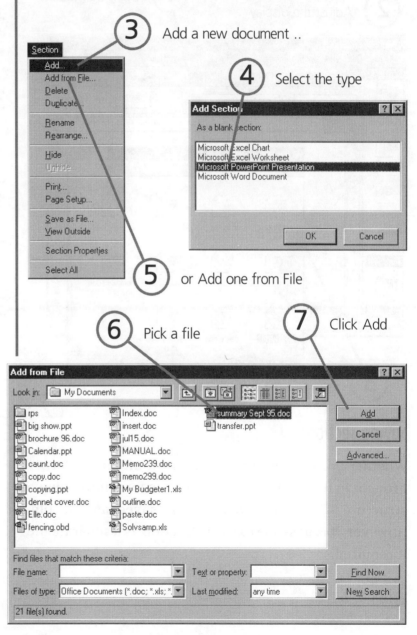

③   Add a new document ..

④   Select the type

⑤   or Add one from File

⑥   Pick a file

⑦   Click Add

Sections and files

If you have a number of files that you want to pull into a binder, it may be quicker to drag them in from their Explorer folder.

(2) Adjust the display

(1) Open the folder

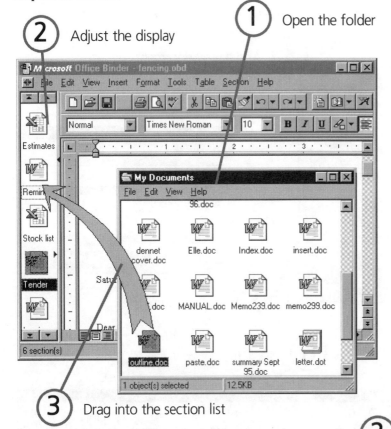

(3) Drag into the section list

Saving sections

Whether the sections were created within the binder, or brought in from file, once in place they form into a single structure – a binder document is saved as one file. However, it is possible to save a section as a separate file if required.

❑ **Dragging files**

1 Run Explorer or My Computer and open the file's folder

2 Adjust the display so that the Binder section pane is in view

3 Drag the file into the Binder, dropping it into place in the list

❑ **Saving sections**

1 Switch to the section

2 Open the **Section** menu and select **Save as File**

3 Complete the **Save** dialog box as normal

(2) Use Section – Save as File

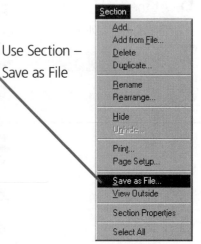

Basic steps

1 Switch to the source document

2 Open the **Section** menu and select **Duplicate**

3 Choose where the new document is to fit

4 Click on the duplicate's name and edit it

④ Names can be edited

③ Where will it go?

Duplicating sections

One of the useful features of binders is that you can easily duplicate a section. For instance, if you wanted several Word documents, all with the same letterhead, you could design the first, then duplicate that document to give you a basis for the others.

① Switch to the document to be copied

② Use Section – Duplicate

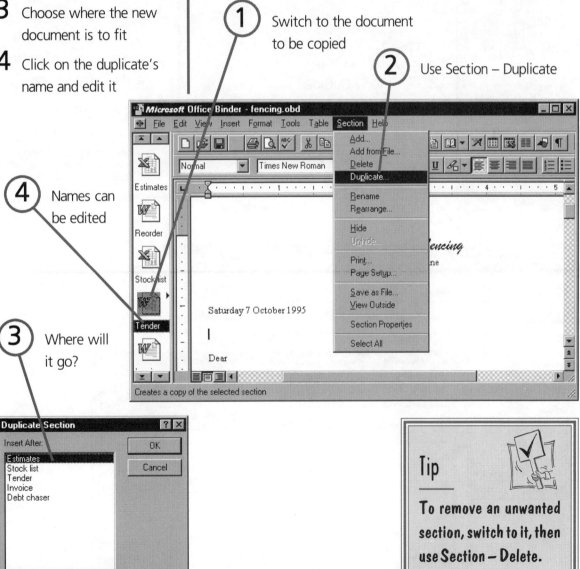

Multiple views

An apparent drawback to the binder is that it can only display one section at a time. There is a simple way round this. The View Outside facility lets you open a free-standing copy of the application to handle a section.

Basic steps

1 Switch to the section you want to view

2 Open the **Section** menu and select **View Outside**

3 Adjust the screen as necessary, so that you can work in the binder and outside section

4 Close down the outside application when you have done – the section will be updated automatically

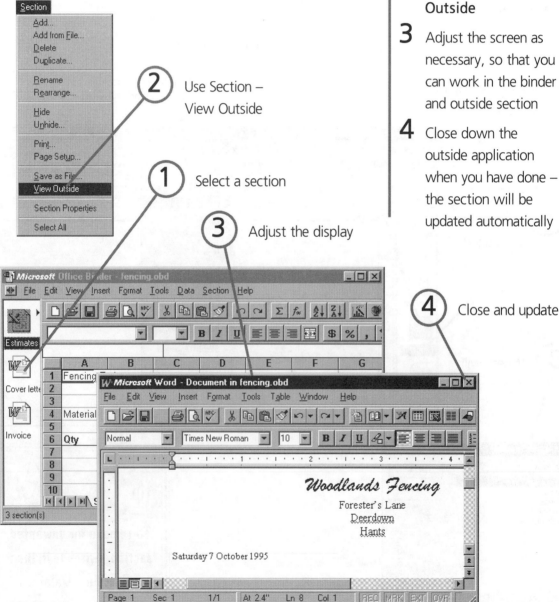

② Use Section – View Outside

① Select a section

③ Adjust the display

④ Close and update

Printing

1 Click on a section to be printed

2 Hold **[Ctrl]** and click the other sections

3 Open the **File** menu and select **Print Binder**

4 Set the **Print What** option to **All** or **Selected sections**

5 Set the **Numbering** to **Continuous** or **Restart each section**

6 Click **OK**

You can print all the sections of the binder at once or select one or more for printing. If you are printing a selection, this must be set up first.

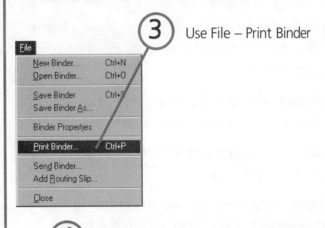

③ Use File – Print Binder

④ Print All or a Selection

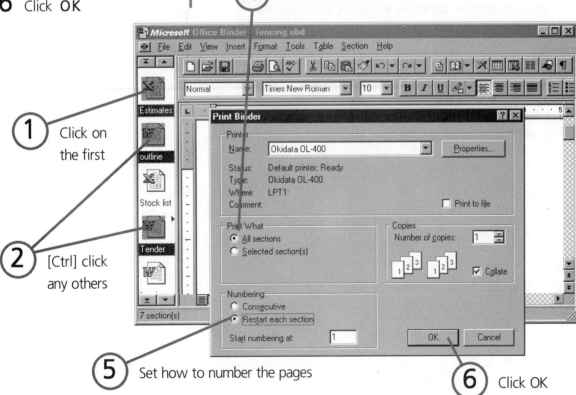

① Click on the first

② [Ctrl] click any others

⑤ Set how to number the pages

⑥ Click OK

Summary

- A **Binder** holds a set of documents from the same or different applications.

- The documents in binders are referred to as **sections.**

- An **empty Binder window** is little more than a frame with a small section of commands for opening binders and adding sections.

- An **application window**, within a binder, has a Section menu and panel on the left side holding section icons.

- There are a few **ready made binders** that can form a useful base for your own.

- **New binders** are created by pulling in existing files or creating new documents from withiin the binder.

- Sections can be **saved as separate files** if needed.

- If you need to see more than one section at a time, the **View Outside** feature lets you open a separate copy of an application to edit a section.

- You can **print** the whole binder or one or more selected sections in one operation.

8 Mail merge

The form letter

Mail merging is a good example of integration between applications. A form letter is created within Word, and contains *fields* into which data will drawn. The data – typically names and addresses – can be in an Access database, Excel table or even your (Exchange) Address Book or Schedule+ Contacts list.

There is a Mail Merge Helper to take you through the process. You can start this up before or after you create the form letter. I like to get the letter written first.

1 Type out and format your letter, leaving blank lines – or a couple of spaces within lines – for the data fields

2 Open the **Tools** menu and select **Mail Merge** to start the **Helper**

3 Under **Mail Document** click [Create ▼] and select **Form Letter**

1 Create the basic document

4 At the prompt select [Active Window]

Leave blank lines for the address

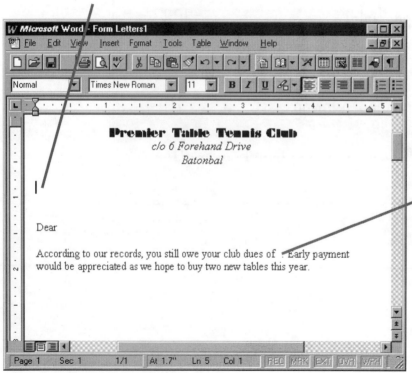

Leave a couple of spaces where fields are to be inserted

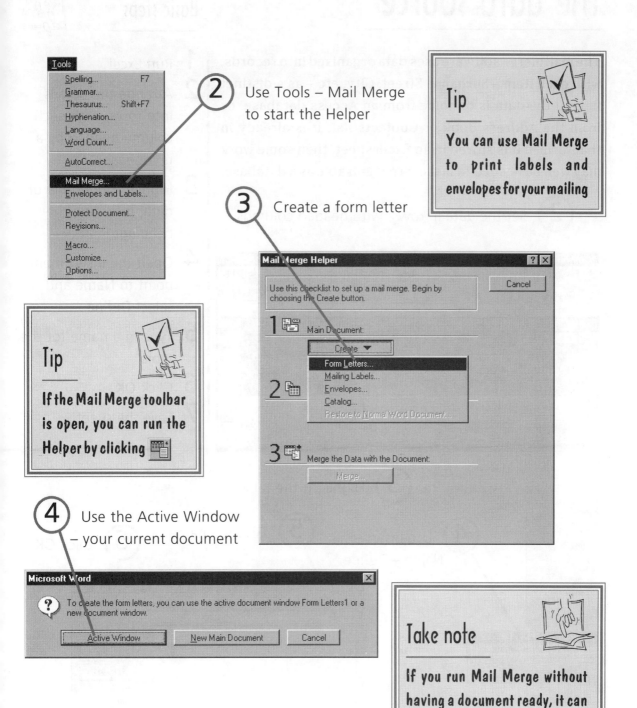

Tools

Spelling...	F7
Grammar...	
Thesaurus...	Shift+F7
Hyphenation...	
Language...	
Word Count...	
AutoCorrect...	
Mail Merge...	
Envelopes and Labels...	
Protect Document...	
Revisions...	
Macro...	
Customize...	
Options...	

② Use Tools – Mail Merge to start the Helper

Tip

You can use Mail Merge to print labels and envelopes for your mailing

③ Create a form letter

Mail Merge Helper

Use this checklist to set up a mail merge. Begin by choosing the Create button.

Cancel

1. Main Document:

    Create ▼

    Form Letters...
    Mailing Labels...
    Envelopes...
    Catalog...
    Restore to Normal Word Document...

2.

3. Merge the Data with the Document:

    Merge...

Tip

If the Mail Merge toolbar is open, you can run the Helper by clicking

④ Use the Active Window – your current document

Microsoft Word

? To create the form letters, you can use the active document window Form Letters1 or a new document window.

| Active Window | New Main Document | Cancel |

Take note

If you run Mail Merge without having a document ready, it can be created at this point.

The data source

The mail merge software uses data organised into records, with each item – Surname, Street, City, etc – as a distinct field. If the data is to come from an Access database, or from the Address Book or Contacts list, it is already in that form. If it is stored in an Excel sheet, then some work may well be needed to make it recognisable as a database.

Basic steps

1 Run Excel

2 Arrange the details into rows, with each column headed by a unique label

3 Highlight the table of data, including the headings

4 Open the **Insert** menu, point to **Name** and select **Define**

5 Type in a name for the table

6 Click **OK**

7 Save the sheet

(2) Set the data in rows, with headed columns

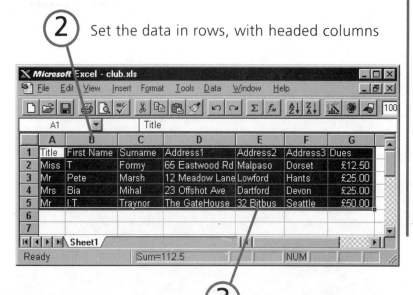

(3) Highlight the table

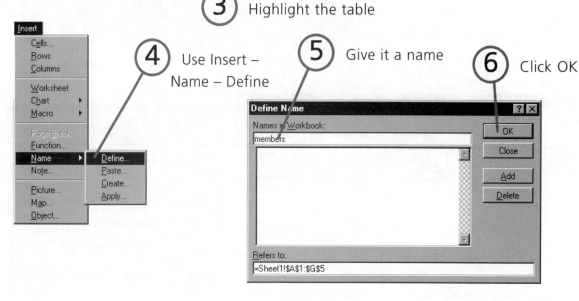

(4) Use Insert – Name – Define

(5) Give it a name

(6) Click OK

Basic steps

1 Restart **Mail Merge Helper** if necessary

2 Under **Data Source** click [Get Data ▼] and select **Open Data Source**

3 The usual **Open File** dialog box starts. Find and open the file

4 Select the **Named range** and click **OK**

Getting the data

Back in Word, the Mail Merge Helper will lead you through the next stage of the process.

(1) Run the Helper

(2) Select Open Data Source

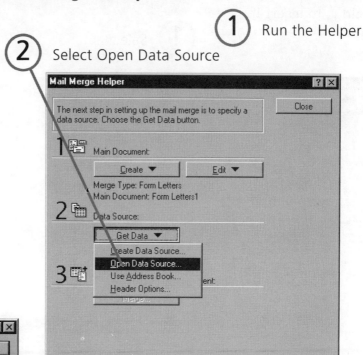

(4) Select the range

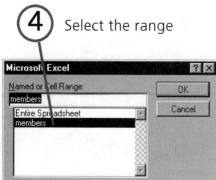

If the sheet only contains the headed table of data, then selecting **Entire Spreadsheet** works just as well

Take note

If you like, the data can be stored in a table in Word. The Create Data Source option leads you through the process of setting up the data and takes you into a Data Form for collecting the information. If you take this route, don't forget to save the Word document with the data.

Inserting fields

Merge fields appear in documents like this – <<Name>>. Don't try to type them in. The only way to create a merge field is to insert it.

Basic steps

1 Under **Main Document**, click ___Edit ▼___ and select the form letter

2 Position the cursor where you want a field

3 Click [Insert Merge Field]

4 Select the field from the drop down list

5 Repeat steps 2 to 4 to place all fields

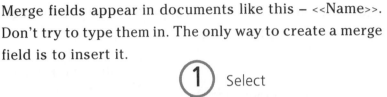

(1) Select

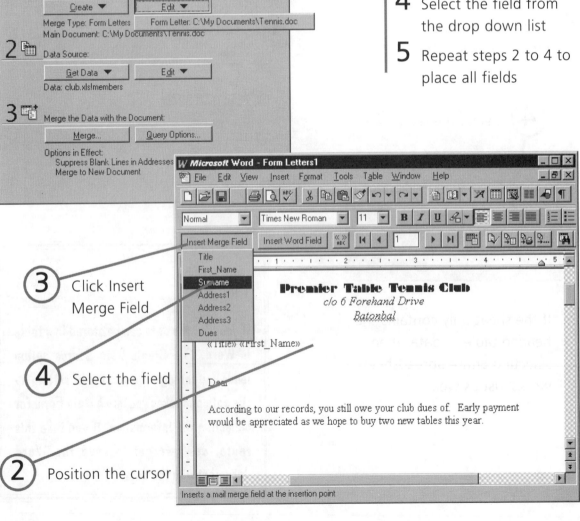

(3) Click Insert Merge Field

(4) Select the field

(2) Position the cursor

Basic steps

1 Click [Merge...] on the **Helper** or [⊡→...] on the toolbar

2 If you only want a limited run, set the **From and To** numbers – these depend on their postion in the data source

3 When printing onto structured forms, you may get better results by printing blank lines for empty fields

4 Click [Query Options...]

❑ **Sorting**

5 Open the **Sort** tab

6 Drop down the **Sort by** list and select the key field

7 Set sort direction

8 Repeat steps 6 and 7 if a second level sort is needed – e.g. sort by *Surname* then *Initials*

Merge options

If you simply want to print out a letter for everyone in the data list, then you can skip straight past the options. But have a look at them now, if only to see what is there.

● **Sort** the file if you want the output in name, status, postcode or other order

● **Filter** to select those who live in certain towns, have A-H names, owe money or match other criteria

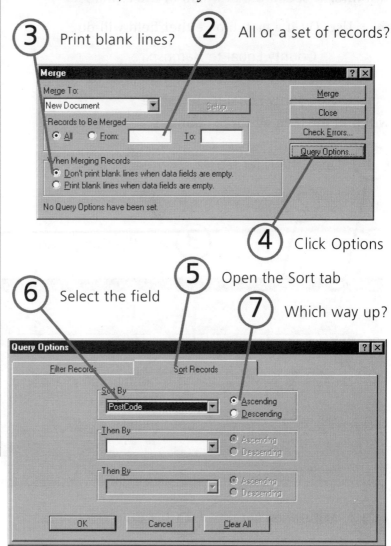

③ Print blank lines? ② All or a set of records?

④ Click Options

⑤ Open the Sort tab

⑥ Select the field

⑦ Which way up?

Filters

As you can set up to six criteria, these can get quite complicated. Where there is more than one, the criteria must be linked by AND or OR in the far left column.

● Use AND if both must be true

> Last_Name Greater than or Equal to A
> AND Last_Name Less than N

will filter those in the first half of the alphabet

● Use OR if a match on either field will do

> County Equal to Hampshire
> OR County Equal to Buckinghamshire
> OR County Equal to Berkshire

will find those in all three counties

Basic steps

❑ **Setting up a filter**

1 Open the **Filter** tab

2 Drop down the **Field** list and select the one to be checked

3 Pick a **Comparison** type – Equal to, Greater than, Less than or a combination

4 Enter the **Compare to** criteria

5 Repeat steps 2 to 4 if you have more than one criterion, setting the AND or OR link

6 Click **OK**

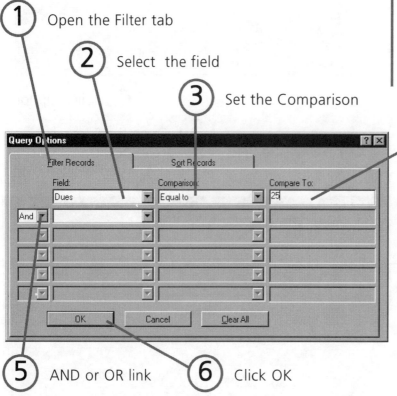

① Open the Filter tab

② Select the field

③ Set the Comparison

④ Enter the match

⑤ AND or OR link

⑥ Click OK

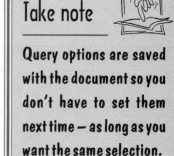

Take note

Query options are saved with the document so you don't have to set them next time – as long as you want the same selection.

Basic steps

❑ **Checking**

1 Click 🔤 to replace the <<fields>> with real data

2 If there are problems with the layout, edit the form letter

3 Click 📝 on the toolbar, or `Check Errors...` on the Helper

4 If errors are reported, you will probably need to edit the data source

❑ **Merging**

5 Click 🖨 to output directly to the printer

or

6 Click 📄 to create a merge document

Before you merge the letter and the data source, check the appearance with the View tool, and run the Check for Errors routine to scan the whole data source.

When you are happy that everything is in order, start the final merging, either direct to the printer, or to another document, for later printing.

① Click View

② View the layout

③ Check for errors

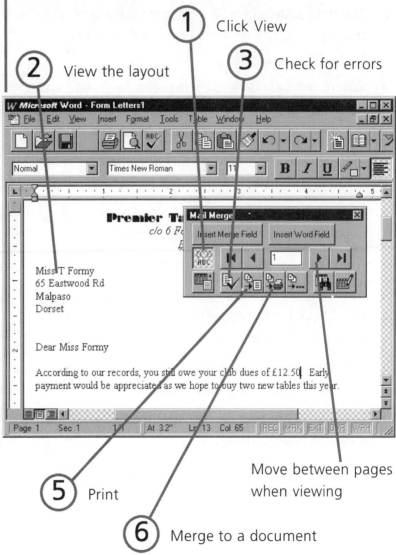

⑤ Print

Move between pages when viewing

⑥ Merge to a document

Take note

A merge document will contain one copy of the form letter for every record in the data source – it could be huge!

Summary

- In a **typical mail merge**, names, address and other details from a database are combined with a standard letter to produce individual letters to each person in the database.

- The **form letter** contains text and merge fields into which actual data will be dropped at output.

- The **data source** can be an Access database, Excel spreadsheet, the Address Book or Schedule+ Contacts list.

- Where the data is held in a spreadsheet, you would normally only use the **named range** that contains the data and the field (column) headings.

- Merge fields can only be placed in the document through the **Insert – Merge fields** routine.

- The database can be **sorted** before merging if you need the output in a particular order.

- **Filters** can be set to select those records match given criteria.

- The **Check for Errors** feature will check that the merge can be done successfully.

- The layout, with real data rather than <<fields>> can be seen with the **View** button.

- The merged **output** can be sent to the printer, or to a file for later printing.

9 Working with Graphics

Importing images

"A picture is worth a thousand words." That's the philosophy of these books, and one that can be applied to many types of documents.

- Your logo on letterheads and invoices will make your company instantly identifiable.

- Pictures of your products in your catalogues should sell them better than any description.

- Diagrams are often essential for communicating technical information and other complex concepts.

Basic steps

- ❏ Pictures in Word

1 Open the **Insert** menu and select **Picture**

2 Switch to the picture's folder

3 Set the **File type** to suit the graphic file

4 Pick a picture, checking its preview

5 Click **OK**

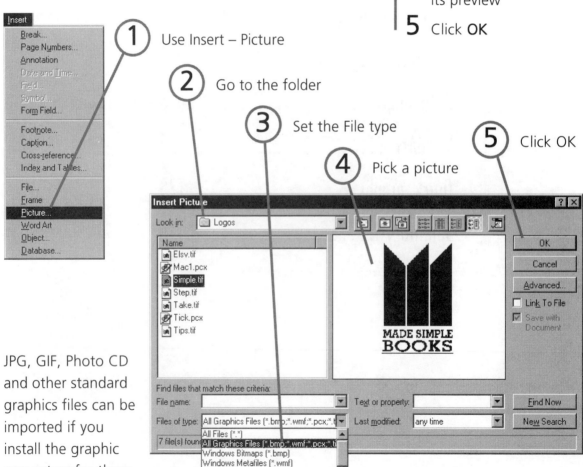

JPG, GIF, Photo CD and other standard graphics files can be imported if you install the graphic converters for them

114

Basic steps

1 Open the **Insert** menu and select **Object**

2 At the **Insert Object** dialog box, select **ClipArt Gallery**

3 Choose a **Category**

4 Scroll through the pictures and select one that suits

5 Click [Insert]

The ClipArt Gallery

Pictures from the ClipArt Gallery can be inserted into any Office application. But don't overdo it. There's so much clip art around that you must use it selectively if you want it to have any impact.

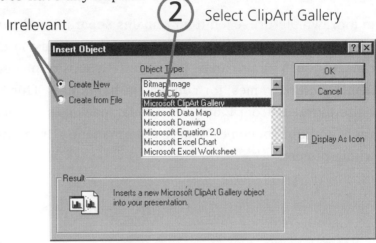

Irrelevant

② Select ClipArt Gallery

③ Choose a Category ④ Pick a picture ⑤ Click Insert

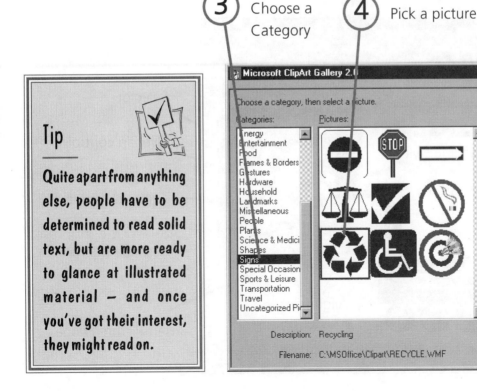

Tip

Quite apart from anything else, people have to be determined to read solid text, but are more ready to glance at illustrated material — and once you've got their interest, they might read on.

Creating diagrams

If you want to create new diagrams or images, pick out points on imported pictures, or simply add arrows, blobs or blocks of background colour, there is a handy set of tools on the Drawing toolbar.

In a drawn picture, each item remains separate and can be moved, resized, recoloured or deleted at any later time. (Though items can be joined into Groups or placed inside picture frames, for convenient handling.) This is quite different from Paint and similar packages, where each addition becomes merged permanently into the whole picture.

Basic steps

1 Click ◢ to open the **Drawing** toolbar

2 Select an object tool and point and drag to create the item

3 Adjust the fill and line colour and style

4 To adjust an existing item, click the Selector tool and click on the item. It can then be moved, deleted, resized or recoloured

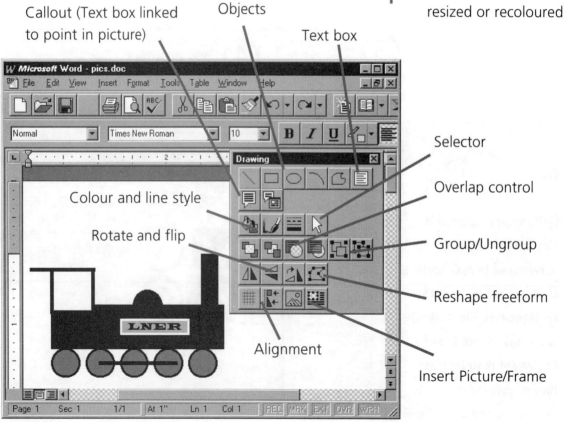

Callout (Text box linked to point in picture)

Objects

Text box

Colour and line style

Rotate and flip

Selector

Overlap control

Group/Ungroup

Reshape freeform

Alignment

Insert Picture/Frame

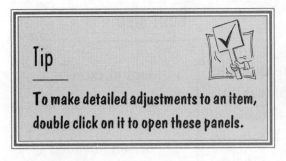
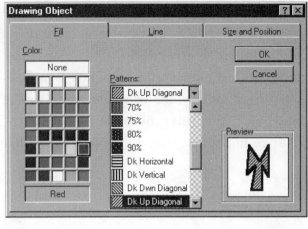

On the **Fill** panel, the percentage shading can be used to create the effect of different colours, (the second colour selector is under the dropped-down pattern list). Other patterns can make objects stand out.

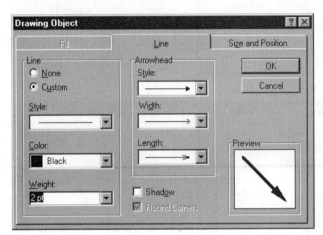

The **Line** panel lets you add arrowheads in a range of styles and sizes, as well as giving you more control over the type and thickness of the line itself.

The **Size and Position** panel is mainly useful for technical diagrams, where accurate placing is important.

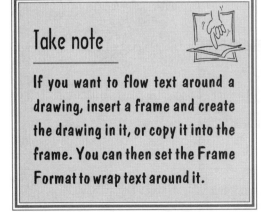
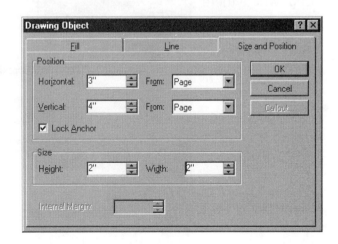

Data maps

One of the clever little extras included in the Office 95 package is the Data Map software – actually, not that little as it occupies over 6Mb. This can take a table of geographical names and associated values – a Sales by Country summary, for example – and use it to create a map, with the relevant places shaded to show their relative importance. And it does it all by itself!

Basic steps

☐ **Maps in Excel**

1 Set up the data with names and values in adjacent, headed columns

2 Select the data range

3 Open the **Insert** menu and select **Map..**

4 Drag an outline for where the map is to go

5 Wait – this could take a couple of minutes

③ Choose Insert – Map..

② Select the data

④ Drag an outline

Relative value indicators
Used where there are several sets of values or to add variety

Shading

Dot density

Graduated symbol

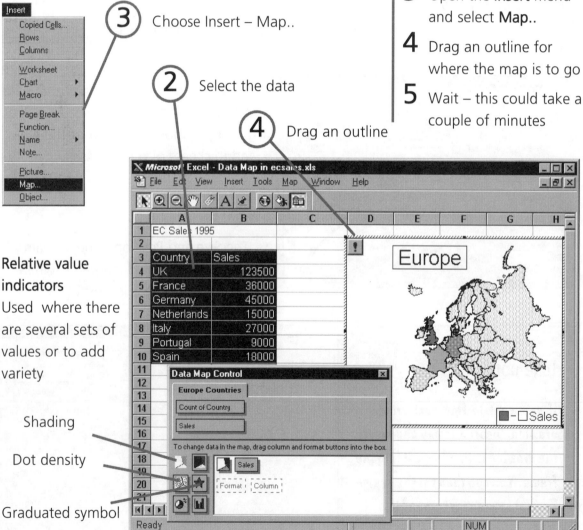

UK Regions

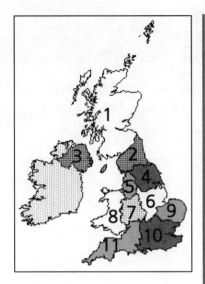

1 Scotland

2 North

3 Northern Ireland

4 Yorkshire and Humberside

5 North West

6 East Midlands

7 West Midlands

8 East Anglia

9 Wales

10 South East UK

11 South West UK

Potential problems

The Data Map software does have its limitations. It knows about countries, US states and UK regions (as long as you use standard names – see below), but not much else.

At the worst you will see this panel.

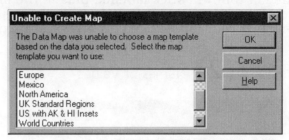

If you do select a map now, it will only be decorative, as the software will not be able to relate your names to any actual places.

You may be given a choice of map. It doesn't matter if one covers too wide an area. You can set the display to zoom in on the relevant part.

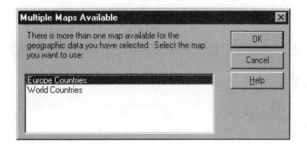

If the software cannot recognise a name, is will ask you for an alternative. For instance, it doesn't know about 'Holland' but will accept 'Netherlands'.

Annotating the map

There are three types of annotations available.

The Label tool will get the names and values from your data table.

The Pin tool will stick labelled pins in the map.

The Text tool can be used for any other text.

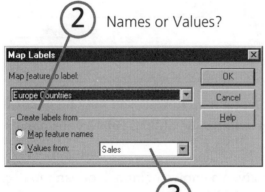

② Names or Values?

③ Which set of values?

① Click the Label tool

⑥ Click the Pin tool

❑ **Labels**

1 Click

2 At the **Map Labels** dialog box, select **Names** or **Values**.

3 With **Values**, if there is more than one values column, select the column

4 Position the crosshair pointer over the area to be labelled and click. Repeat as needed

5 Select any other tool to end

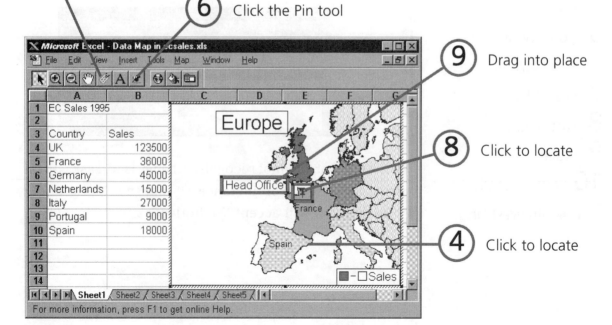

⑨ Drag into place

⑧ Click to locate

④ Click to locate

120

6 Click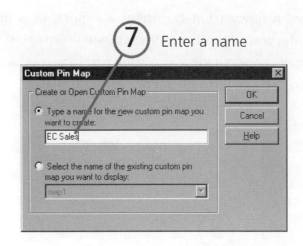

7 At the **Custom Pin Map** dialog box, give a name for the file that will be created

8 Click to place a pin, then type its label

9 Drag the pin to move both together, or the label to move it alone

⑦ Enter a name

Basic steps

1 In Word or PowerPoint use **Insert – Object** and select **Data Map**

2 When the map appears select **Insert – External Data**

3 Open the Access of Excel file, specifying a range if necessary

4 Continue as for an Excel Data Map

Maps in Word and PowerPoint

A Data Map can give impact to a report or presentation. Adding one is much the same as in Excel, with one key exception. When you insert a Map Object, you will get a standard (World) map. You must then link to an Access or Excel table to get the data.

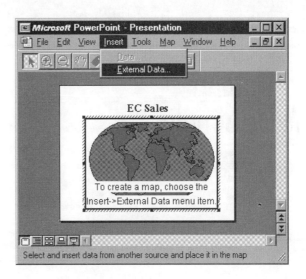

WordArt

If you want a fancy front cover for a report, or a high impact slide, you might like to investigate WordArt. With this, you can shape, shadow and style text in ways that go far beyond the standard Font Formatting tools.

1 Open the **Insert** menu and select **WordArt** (or **Object**, then **WordArt**)

2 Enter your text at the prompt. It can run onto several lines if wanted

3 Select the font and size – **Best Fit** selects a size to suit the outline, and will adjust if the outline is resized

4 Set Bold and other effects if required

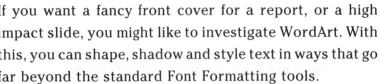

① Use Insert – WordArt

③ Set the font and size

④ Set other effects

Bold   All letters the same size

Italics

② Type the text   Rotate 90°

Stretch to fill outline

Centre Alignment

Character spacing

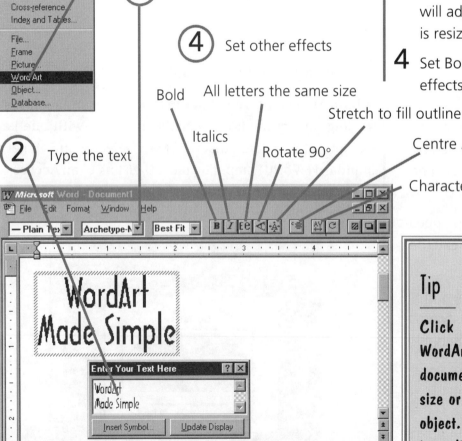

Tip

Click outside the WordArt to return to the document to change the size or position of the object. Double click on it to edit in WordArt.

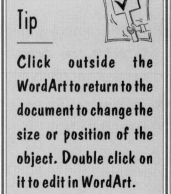

❑ **Setting the shape**

5 Drop down the shape palette

6 Select the basic shape – you may need to try several before you find one that works for you

7 Click 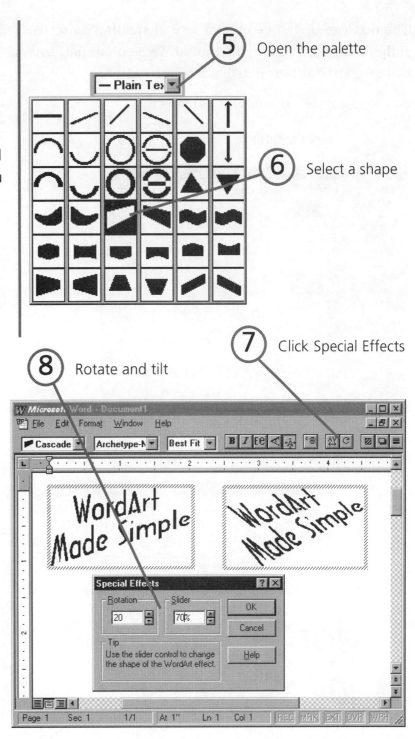 to open the **Special Effects** dialog box

8 Set the **Rotation** to turn the text; **Slider** to change the angle of the letters

The example on the left has 0° Rotation and 50% Slider – the default for the shape. The one on the right has 20° Rotation and 50% Slider. If you rotate, it is usually better to adjust the tilt.

⑤ Open the palette

⑥ Select a shape

⑦ Click Special Effects

⑧ Rotate and tilt

Shading and Shadows

The text can be in one of a variety of shading patterns, rather than solid colour, if required. Two-colour patterns can give striking – or garish – effects.

Shadows can be added for a 3-D effect.

(2) Select a pattern   (3) Pick a colour

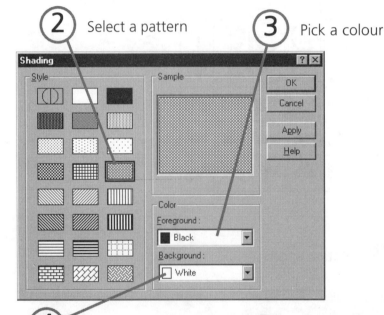

(4) Set for two-colour pattern   (6) Choose a style

(7) Shadow colour?

Basic steps

- ❏ **Shading**
- **1** Click
- **2** Select a pattern
- **3** Set the Foreground
- **4** For a two-colour pattern, change the Background from White

- ❏ **Shadow**
- **5** Click
- **6** Select a shadow style
- **7** Set the shadow colour

Tip

WordArt headings look better in solid and in black or other rich colour. WordArt used as a background to other text should be in a pale colour or lightly patterned black.

Basic steps

1 Open the **Insert** menu, select **Object** then **Graph 5.0**

2 Replace the headings and data in the datasheet, expanding into more columns or rows if needed

3 Use the tools to change the display, if desired – most toggle features on and off

4 Click back into the document and adjust the graph's size

Tip

To change the colour or fill pattern of a series of bars, select them all by clicking on any one of them – if you see a highlight block in each, they are selected.

If you want to knock up a quick graph in a Word or PowerPoint document, the Graph5 software will do the job. It gives you a datasheet and related graph, set up with dummy data. All you have to do is replace that data with your own. If you care to spend the time, you can also change the chart style, colours and other aspects of its appearance.

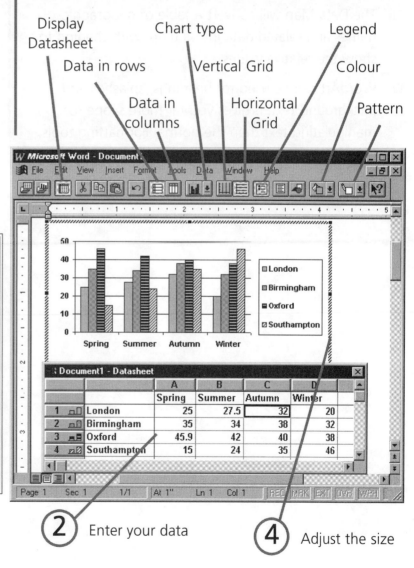

Display Datasheet · Data in rows · Data in columns · Chart type · Vertical Grid · Horizontal Grid · Legend · Colour · Pattern

	Spring	Summer	Autumn	Winter
London	25	27.5	32	20
Birmingham	35	34	38	32
Oxford	45.9	42	40	38
Southampton	15	24	35	46

2 Enter your data

4 Adjust the size

Summary

❑ You can import **clipart**, **pictures** and other images in most common graphics formats into any Office application, to illustrate or enhance a document.

❑ There is a set of varied images in the **ClipArt Gallery**.

❑ The **Drawing** tools can be used to creat diagrams or add lines, arrows or other simple graphics.

❑ The **Data Map** will convert a table of geographic names and related data into a map, with shading to show the relative values.

❑ **WordArt** can be used for headings, splashes and background text. It gives you far more scope for manipulating text than the normal Formatting tools.

❑ To produce a graph from a small table of data quickly, insert a **Graph** object.

10 Schedule+

Starting up

Schedule+ can be used as a personal organiser, but if you are on a local or extended network it can also be used for arranging meetings of group members. It has three main elements:

- A list of **Contact** names, addresses, phone and fax numbers, with a handy built-in phone dialler.

- A **Planner**/appointments calendar, with a reminder facility.

- A **Things To Do** list, for scheduling tasks and monitoring their progress.

The three elements can be interrelated, linking tasks to contacts or meetings, and contacts to meetings.

Take note

The Contacts list in Schedule and the Address Book in Exchange cannot share their data. Until some clever person comes up with a way to export a file from one and import it into the other, you'll just have to retype the data. Irritating, isn't it?

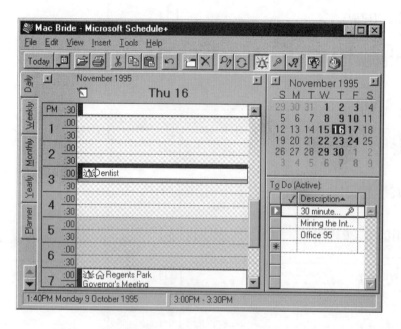

All three elements can be viewed in a variety of ways. For example, the calendar can be displayed on a yearly, monthly, weekly or daily basis. The example here has a multiple view, showing the day, the month and the current To Do list.

You can choose which view to use – see page 131

Basic steps

□ **The Schedule file**

1 Enter your name

2 Select **Create a new schedule file**

3 Unless you need to store it in another folder, accept the default settings at the **Save** dialog box

□ **Group enabling**

4 If you are on a network, when you next start Schedule, you can opt to work in group mode

Initial set-up

The first couple of times that you use Schedule+, there will be some little chores to do.

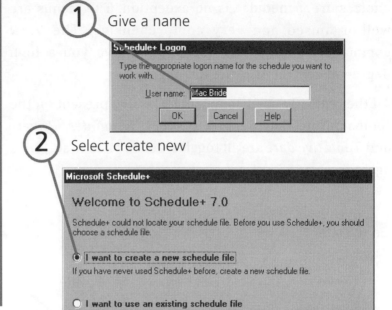

① Give a name

② Select create new

③ Accept the defaults

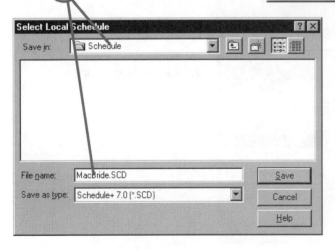

④ Group or single user?

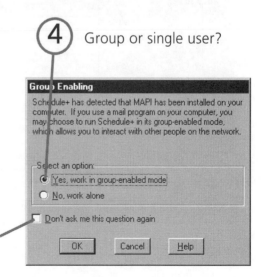

If you always work the same way, set the mode then click here

The Schedule+ tools

With most Windows software, it is often easier at first to work from the menus, as they show you clearly what your choices are. Schedule+ is no exception. The menus are well-organised and very comprehensive. The View commands, for instance (see right), give you a high degree of control over the display.

All the regularly used commands are also present on the toolbar. Note that *Recurring event*, *Reminder*, *Private* and *Tentative date* are all toggles – click once to set, click again to clear.

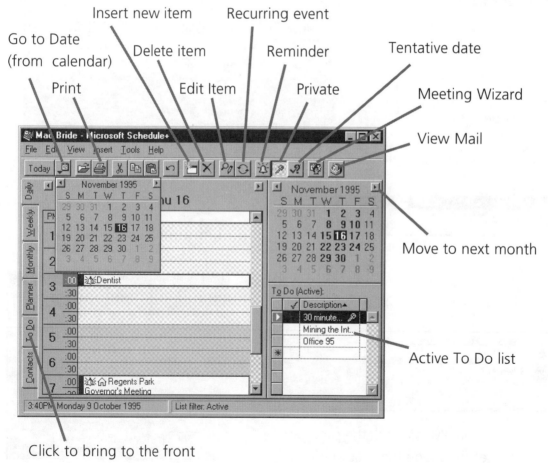

Go to Date (from calendar)

Print

Insert new item

Delete item

Edit Item

Recurring event

Reminder

Private

Tentative date

Meeting Wizard

View Mail

Move to next month

Active To Do list

Click to bring to the front

Basic steps

1 Open the **View** menu and select **Tab Gallery**

❏ **Adding a tab**

2 Select a tab from the left pane, using the **Preview** and **Description** to get an idea of its display

3 Click [Add ->]

4 Move it up or down as necessary

❏ **Removing a tab**

5 Select a tab from the right pane

6 Click [<- Remove]

Tip

An unwanted tab can be removed from the main display. Select it and use View – Remove Tab.

The Preview is small, but useful. The Description can be incomprehensible if you don't know the jargon

Tabs and views

The default set up has tabs for Daily, Weekly and Monthly diaries, the Planner, To Do list and Contacts. Tabs can be added or removed, to suit your way of working, using the option on the View menu.

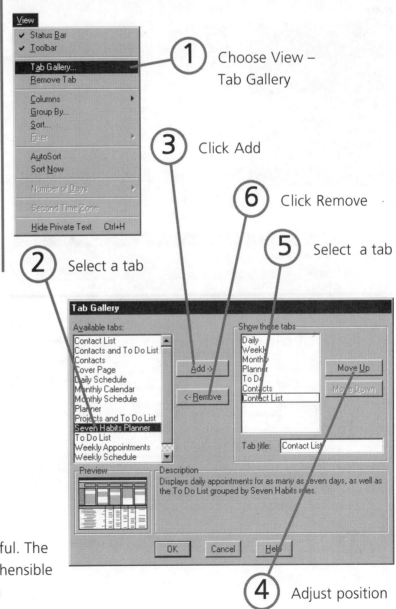

① Choose View – Tab Gallery

③ Click Add

⑥ Click Remove

⑤ Select a tab

② Select a tab

④ Adjust position

The Contacts list

This is probably the most straightforward part of Schedule to set up. Mind you, it will take a while if you give all the details that it can hold – home and business address, phone and fax, birthdays, spouse, assistant, dog's name....

Basic steps

1 Open the **Contacts** tab

2 Open the **Insert** menu and select **Contact**

3 Enter the name and other details, opening tabs as necessary

4 Click **OK**

❑ The new name will be slotted into the list in alphabetical order

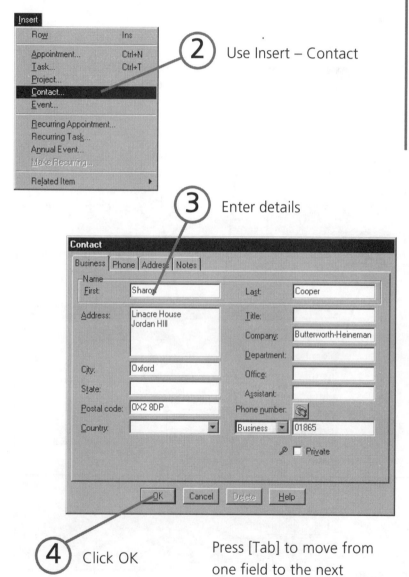

② Use Insert – Contact

③ Enter details

④ Click OK

Press [Tab] to move from one field to the next

Tip

When you are first adding contacts, you can enter the details in the main list display, but they will not put themselves in order. View – Sort will reorganise the list.

Basic steps

1 Open the **Contacts** tab
2 Type the first letter(s) of the last name into the **Go to** slot.
3 Select the person
4 Open the **Phone** tab
5 Click the dialler beside the number you want
6 Lift the phone
7 When the number rings, click [Talk]

Phone dialling

Clicking on [icon] beside a phone numbers will dial the phone for you, if it is connected through the PC's modem.

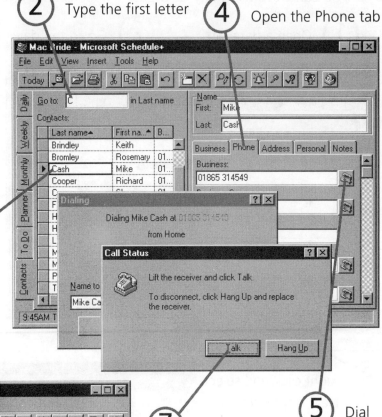

② Type the first letter   ④ Open the Phone tab

③ Select the contact

⑦ Click Talk   ⑤ Dial

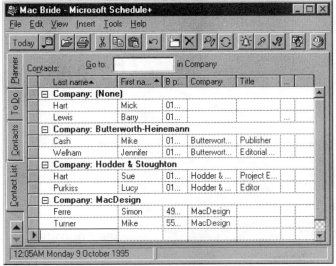

Take note

In the Contact List display, contacts can be grouped by Company, if you have given those details.

Making a date

Appointments are at the heart of Schedule+, and there are a number of optional refinements here.

● You can work from any of the date-based tabs.

Basic steps

Basic steps

1 Open the **Daily, Weekly** or **Monthly** tab

2 Move to the day of the appointment

3 Right click to open the short menu and select **New Appointment**

4 Type the **Start** and **End** times, or highlight the hours/minutes and click the little arrows

5 Enter a **Description**

6 Enter the **Where** location if relevant

7 If you are not setting options, click **OK**

(1) Open a date tab   (2) Go to the day

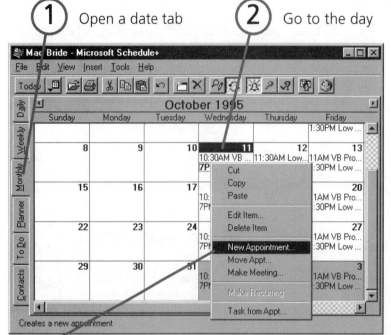

(3) Right click and select New Appointment

(4) Set the times

(5) Enter a Description

(6) Where is it?

See page 136

See opposite

(7) Click OK

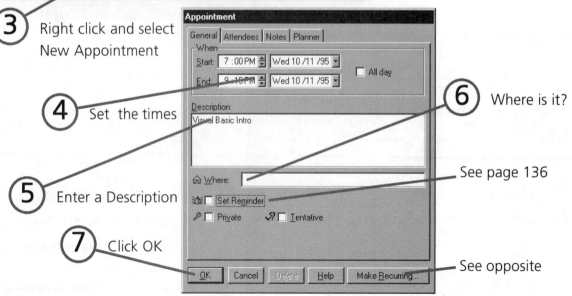

Basic steps

1 Follow steps 1 to 6 opposite to set up the first of the series

2 Click [Make Recurring...]

3 Set the period type

4 Set the day and frequency

5 Check that the **Effective** date is the first of the series

6 If the series has a limited term, check **Until** and select the end date

7 Set the times

8 Click **OK**

Recurring appointments

If you have a series of regular appointments, you can set them all up in one operation.

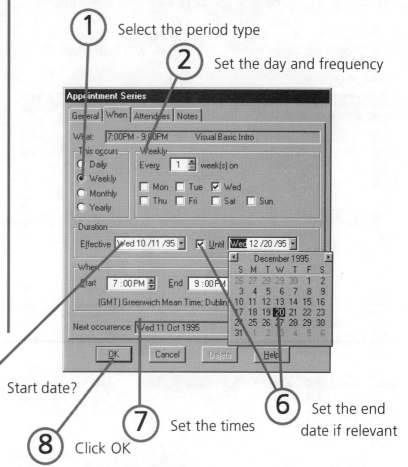

(1) Select the period type

(2) Set the day and frequency

(5) Start date?

(8) Click OK

(7) Set the times

(6) Set the end date if relevant

Take note

There is a different 'regular day' panel for Daily, Monthly and Yearly appointments

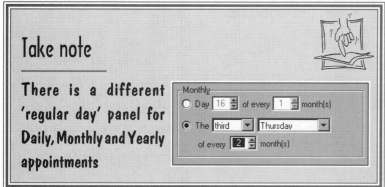

Reminders

These can be set when the appointment is first made, but – as with other details – they can be changed later. Reminders are normally given 15 minutes beforehand.

1 Select the appointment

2 To turn a reminder on or off click 🔔

❑ **Setting the reminder time**

3 Right click on the appointment and select **Edit item**

4 Choose the time period from the drop down list

5 Set how many minutes, hours, days or week notice you want

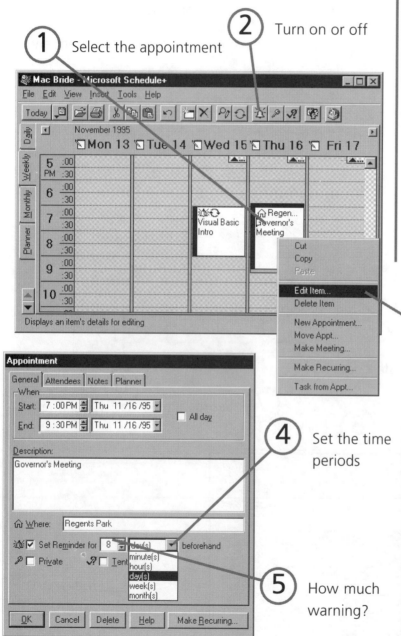

② Turn on or off

① Select the appointment

③ Right click and choose Edit item

④ Set the time periods

⑤ How much warning?

Tip

You only get reminders if Schedule is active. Put a shortcut to it in your Startup folder so that it runs every session.

The Seven Habits

It's a six-step process, though only the first three are covered by the Wizard – but that may be enough.

When you have half an hour to spare, take a look at the Seven Habits Tools (on the Tools menu) – if it is installed. It is a strange mix of common sense and 'better-business' evangelism, but does make you think about your priorities and strategies in both your business and social life.

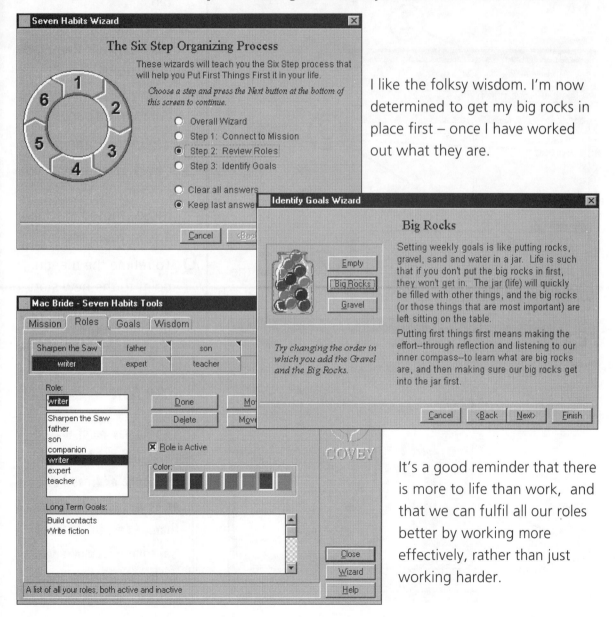

I like the folksy wisdom. I'm now determined to get my big rocks in place first – once I have worked out what they are.

It's a good reminder that there is more to life than work, and that we can fulfil all our roles better by working more effectively, rather than just working harder.

Arranging meetings

This is probably of most use to people who are working on a local area network, where each has access to the (public) diary of the others. However, it can still be a convenient way of calling a meeting with those that you can contact by fax or e-mail.

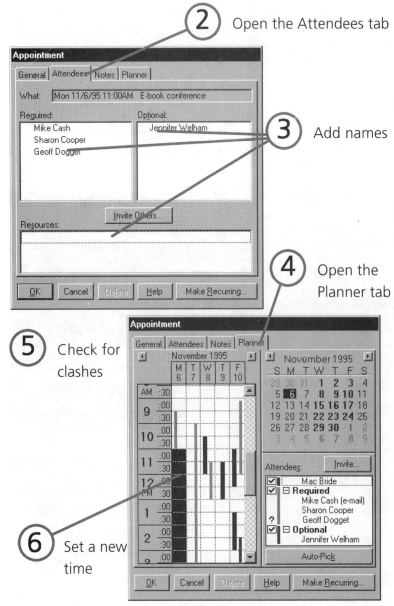

② Open the Attendees tab

③ Add names

④ Open the Planner tab

⑤ Check for clashes

⑥ Set a new time

1 Set up a (tentative) appointment following the steps on page 134

2 Open the **Attendees** tab

3 Enter those whose attendance is **Required** or **Optional**, or will supply **Resources** in the appropriate panes

4 Open the **Planner** tab

5 Check for clashes – you can only do this for those whose Schedules are on your network

6 To retime the meeting, point to the new start and drag the highlight to the end time

Take note

The names must match those in your Microsoft Exchange address book, or be added to it at the time. (Yes, this part of Schedule uses Exchange, not its own Contacts list.)

138

Basic steps

7 When the meeting's details are finished, click **OK**. The **Meeting Request** panel opens

8 The **To**, **Cc** (Copies) and **Subject** lines will have been filled in. To send copies to other people, write their names in the Cc slot, separating them with semi-colons

9 Type a brief note to let people know about the meeting

10 Click 📧 to send the e-mail

---

⑦ The Meeting Request panel opens

⑩ Send it   ⑧ Copy to any others?

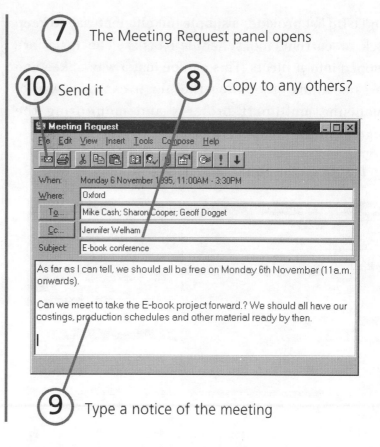

⑨ Type a notice of the meeting

Click 📅 on the Schedule toolbar for the Meeting Wizard

Tip

You can use the Meeting Wizard to work through this process and check for clashes in the Planner — it is easier, but can take a little longer.

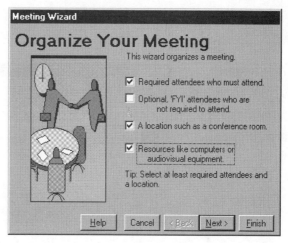

Things to do

The To Do list provides a simple but efficient way to keep track of current and scheduled tasks. The tasks are grouped into *projects*. This can be just a way of keeping the same kinds of jobs together, or it can be a way of organising multi-part projects and monitoring the progress of the component tasks.

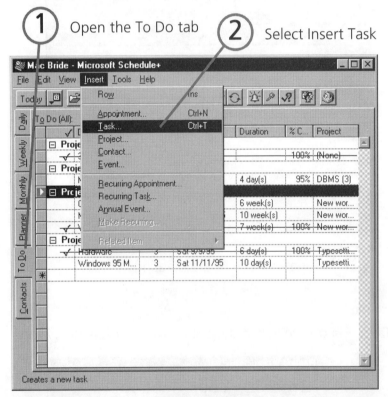

① Open the To Do tab ② Select Insert Task

When Schedule+ starts up it reminds you what needs doing that day

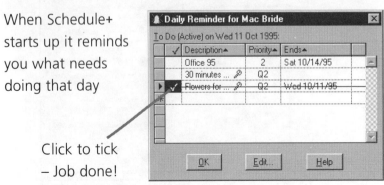

Click to tick
– Job done!

1 Open the **To Do** tab

2 Pull down the **Insert** menu and select **Task** or click

3 On the **General** tab, tick the **Ends** check box, then drop down the calendar and set the completion date

4 Set the **Starts before** in days, weeks or months

5 Type in a **Description**

6 Open the **Status** tab and set the **Estimated effort**

7 If the job is already underway, set the **Percentage complete** and **Actual effort**

8 If the task concerns a **Contact**, drop down the list and select the person

9 Click **OK**

140

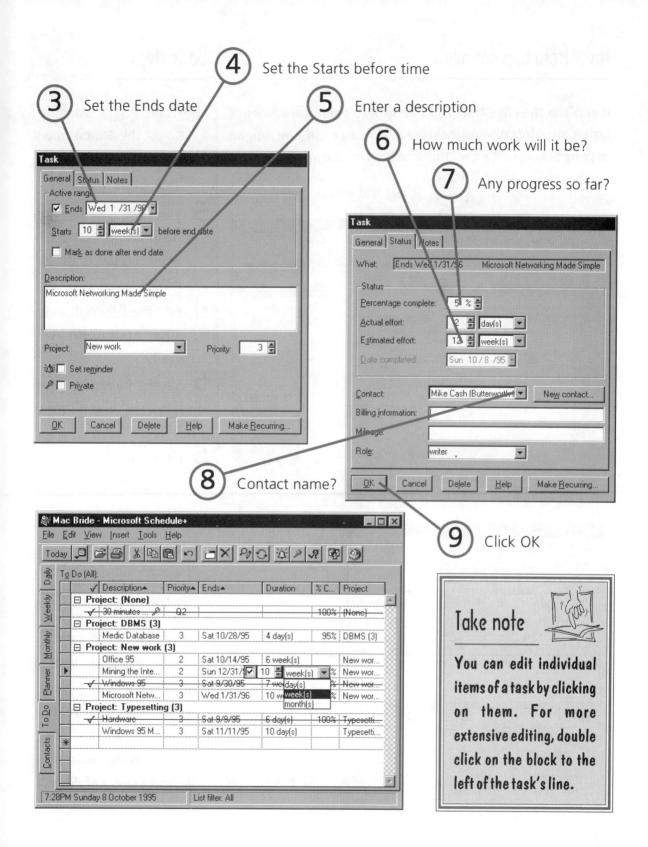

③ Set the Ends date

④ Set the Starts before time

⑤ Enter a description

⑥ How much work will it be?

⑦ Any progress so far?

⑧ Contact name?

⑨ Click OK

Take note

You can edit individual items of a task by clicking on them. For more extensive editing, double click on the block to the left of the task's line.

Tasks from appointments

It is often the case that you need to do preparatory work for an appointment or meeting. This can easily be logged in your Schedule by creating a task from the appointment.

1 Open a date tab and select the appointment

2 Right click and choose **Task from Appt....**

3 The **Ends** date will have been set up, but you need to set the **Starts** before

4 Edit the **Description** to show what needs doing

5 Set the **Reminder** time if wanted – and turn it off, if not

6 Click **OK**

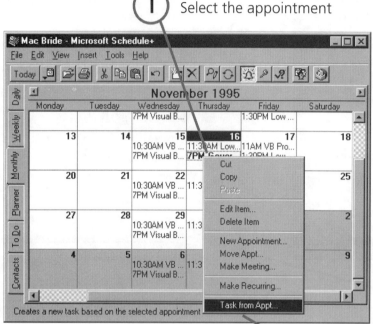

(1) Select the appointment

(2) Pick Task from Appt..

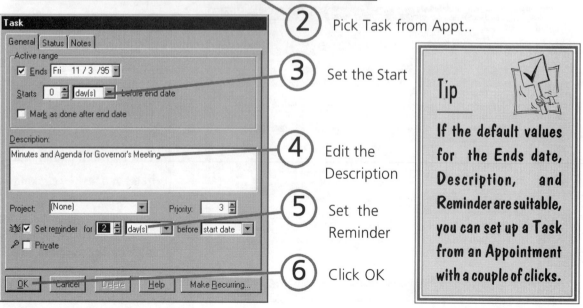

(3) Set the Start

(4) Edit the Description

(5) Set the Reminder

(6) Click OK

Tip

If the default values for the Ends date, Description, and Reminder are suitable, you can set up a Task from an Appointment with a couple of clicks.

Basic steps

❑ **Filtering**

1 Open the **View** menu and point to **Filter**

2 Select the type to display

❑ **Sorting and Grouping**

3 Open the **View** menu and select **Sort.. (or Group..)**

4 Select the first criterion from the list

5 Set the direction – **Ascending** or **Descending**

6 Repeat for the next two levels of sort (or group), if wanted.

The To Do list display

If you are a very busy person, or are just not too good at finishing things off, your To Do list could get crowded. Make the display easier to read, either with a Filter (based on completion status) or by Grouping and Sorting to focus on key tasks.

① Use View – Filter   **②** What to show

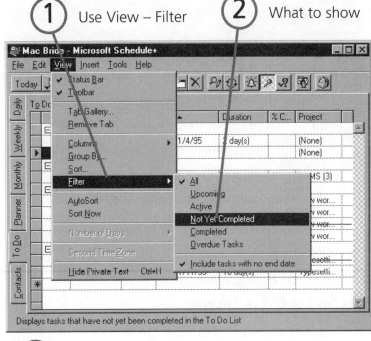

④ Sort by what aspect?

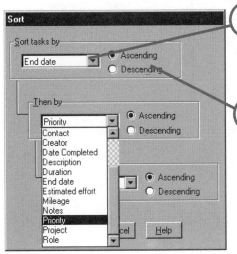

⑤ Which way up

> **Tip**
>
> If you use high numbers to show high Priority, sort in Descending order to bring high Priority tasks to the top.

Summary

❑ Schedule+ is a **personal** and **workgroup organizer** in which you can store contacts, appointments and lists of tasks.

❑ When **first starting up** you will need to specify a filename for your Schedule+ data.

❑ Schedule+ can be run in **single-user** or **group** mode.

❑ You can select the **Tabs** to be included in your display.

❑ The **Contacts list** can be used to record very complete details of your contacts.

❑ You can **dial phone numbers** in your Contacts list by clicking the dialler button.

❑ When adding **appointments**, you can set them to **recur** weekly, monthly or at any fixed interval.

❑ **Reminders** can be set for any time before an appointment.

❑ The **Seven Habits Tools** can help you to arrange your priorities and practices.

❑ People in networked groups can arrange **meetings** through Schedule+. The Meeting Wizard can handle the donkey work for you.

❑ The **To Do list** can be used to schedule activities and to record progress on them. Reminders can be set for time-limited tasks.

Index

Windows 95 Made Simple

Quickly learn what's essential and how to make the computer work for <u>you</u>.

- **easy to follow** - **jargon free** - **practical** - **task based** - **easy steps**

All you need to get you started.

If you're:

✔ a **manager** who needs to **quickly understand Windows 95,** what it can do
   for you and how things differ from Windows 3.1, etc;

✔ a **secretary** who wants to **get the job done**, quickly and efficiently
   using Windows 95;

✔ a person **working from home** who needs a **self-teaching** approach
   that gives **results fast,**

then **Windows 95 Made Simple** is for you !

By a combination of **tutorial approach**, with **tasks to do** and **easy steps**,
the **Made Simple** series of Computer Books stands above all others.

ISBN: 0 7506 2306 3, Sept 95, paperback, 160 pages.

See for yourself why so many people are delighted with this book, and others in the
Made Simple Series, readers comments include:

- 'Clear, concise and well laid out.'
- 'Ideal for the first time user.'
- 'Clear, accurate, well presented, jargon free, well targeted.'
- 'Easy to follow to perform a task.'
- 'Easy to use.'
- 'Illustrations are excellent.'
- 'I haven't found any other books worth recommending until these.'

> Available from all good bookshops, or in case of difficulty, contact:
> Reed Book Services Ltd, Orders Dept, PO Box 5, Rushden, Northants, NN10 9YX.
> Tel: 01933 58521; Fax: 01933 50284; Credit Card Sales Hotline: 01933 414000.

The Internet Made Simple

All you need to get you started.

If you want to know how to:

✔ **set up hardware and software to get on-line**
✔ **find the best service provider for your needs**
✔ **send e-mail, read the news and download files from around the world**
✔ **explore the World Wide Web**

then **The Internet Made Simple** is for you !

By a combination of **tutorial approach**, with **tasks to do** and **easy steps**, the **Made Simple** series of Computer Books stands above all others.

ISBN: 0 7506 2311 X, April 95, paperback, 160 pages.

Readers comments on **The Internet Made Simple** include:

● 'An excellent book. Congratulations to the Author.'

● 'It's not that often that I find a computer book that has been informative as well as enjoyable to read. Your book has enabled me to understand the Internet at least to a level that I can start to explore without fear.'

● 'After buying what seemed like a hundred books on Internet access I eventually acquired your "*Internet Made Simple*" and found it far more helpful than anything else I had previously waded through. I have everything up and running well and feel quite pleased I've survived the steep learning curve. Thank you.'

● 'Thankyou for saving my sanity with your excellent, clear, concise book on the Internet. I browsed through dozens of books, none of which seemed right, before choosing yours. Nice to read something so clear, up-to-date, focused on the kind of software I was using and not biased towards the US !!'

Available from all good bookshops, or in case of difficulty, contact:
Reed Book Services Ltd, Orders Dept, PO Box 5, Rushden, Northants, NN10 9YX.
Tel: 01933 58521; Fax: 01933 50284; Credit Card Sales Hotline: 01933 414000.